FEDERAL PARTY OF MANIPUR (1993-2000) A.D.

Naorem Joykumar Singh

AKANSHA PUBLISHING HOUSE

NEW DELHI-110002

AKANSHA PUBLISHING HOUSE
4649-B/21, Ansari Road
Darya Ganj, New Delhi - 110 002
Email: ektabooks@yahoo.com
Ph.: 23263193/9811582579

FEDERAL PARTY OF MANIPUR (1993-2000)

First Published 2006
ISBN—81-8370-047-0

PRINTED IN INDIA

Published by M.P. Misra for Akansha Publishing House, New Delhi and Printed at Tarun Offset Press, Delhi

SHRI NAOREM BIRENDRAKUMAR SINGH
PRESIDENT OF THE PUBLIC MEETING HELD ON
21ST SEPTEMBER 1993

PROF. GANGMUMEI KAMEI
FOUNDER PRESIDENT
FEDERAL PARTY OF MANIPUR

PROF. NAOREM JOYKUMAR SINGH
FOUNDER GENERAL SECRETARY
FEDERAL PARTY OF MANIPUR

In Memory
of
My Beloved Mother
Late NAOREM IBETOMBI DEVI

CONTENTS

	Preface	xi
1.	Prelude	1
2.	Parturition	19
3.	Legitimization of the organization	34
4.	Participation in the art of governance	58
5.	Involvement in public issues.	81
6.	New Frontrunner	105
7.	Conclusion	115
	Appendices	125
	Bibliography	138
	Index	141

PREFACE

Right from the beginning of 20th century the people of Manipur had enjoyed an opportunity to witness the nature of the working system of the political parties. It is a fact that the birth of political parties is a direct outcome of the maturity of the growth of political consciousness among the people of the state and it produced a very good substantial impact on the political life of the state. Manipur state is indeed, a creation of many trial and errors in the course of her history. To reach to the position of nation stage in the 18th century from a very fragmentary stage of tribalism is not a matter of sheer luck. It was a great contribution of the people of this state. From the last part of the 19th century she again witnessed a new system of colonial administration under British. Then with the introduction of new education system the people began to imbuse with the modern political consciousness and gradually the idea for a distinctive political identity was emerged in the minds of the people. Ultimately it led to the birth of political parties for the strengthening of a new political system based on democratic principle. Thus the political parties played a very important role in moulding the minds of the people for a better future of the state.

Many books have been published by different writers on the history of the political parties. From these writings people came to be aware of the objectives, ideologies, principles and participation of various political parties in the governance of the state and their involvement in the welfare of the people. Thus through these books people are able to assess the positive contribution which they rendered for the strengthening of the moral standard of the common people in a democratic set up.

But so far, as Manipur is concerned unfortunately still people are not able to see any book written on the history of political parties in a more analytical way. It is true that Manipur has a very good experience of the working of the political parties but due to lack of documented paper works the common people are not fully aware of the nature of working of these political parties and their political participation in the governance of the state. Now a new trend has emerged in the state under which many young researchers are trying to understand nature of working of the political parties in the state with an objective. to visualize the possible future course of political trend of the state and people.

Seeing the dearth of even the non-availability of well-research works on the history of the political parties and considering the immediate need for such kind of work I thought that if some attempt is made on this area which could be a great contribution to further research. Keeping this view into consideration I have selected the 'Federal Party of Manipur' as a topic of my work. So far as my knowledge is concerned, this party has a distinctive objective, ideology and agenda which are drastically different from other political parties. The objective and agenda of this political party is quite relevant to this present political scenario particularly in the context of the mainstream of Indian. I believe polities also that in future many research workers who intend to work on the same field would make a serious attempt to analyse working value of other political parties.

In the process of the preparation of this book I took help and suggestions from many close comrades of different disciplines. Specially I would like to express my sincere thanks to the office assistance of Federal Party of Manipur for providing me all possible facilities. I also thank both the staff members of the Centre for Manipur Studies and the Office of the Dean of Social Sciences for their full co-operation. My thanks also go to Dr. S. Amal Singh, Shri K. Meghachandra Singh and Shri A. Koireng Singh for their physical contribution and moral encouragement in the process of the final preparation of this book. I am also fully convinced that without the sincere help of my family members I will not be able to complete my task. The successful completion of my work was made possible only with the help of my wife and children. Therefore, I also thank the members of my family for their sincere help.

Lastly, I also thank Shri M.P. Misra, the Proprietor of Akansha Publishing House whom I always consider a motivating force for my academic work for his kind acceptance to publish the book.

N. JOYKUMAR SINGH

CHAPTER ONE

PRELUDE

The first part of the twentieth century was a significant period in the political history of Manipur. Indeed, it may be treated as the gestation period for the emergence of the idea of the establishment of political parties in the state. The concept of political party was a direct outcome of the maturity of the growth of political consciousness among the common people of Manipur. The year 1934 may be marked as the year of the attainment of the maturity of the growth of political consciousness in the state. The birth of the 'Nikhil Hindu Manipuri Mahasabha' as a socio-religious organization with an objective to promote the idea of pan-Manipuri identity may be treated as the foundation stone for the birth of political parties in the state. The concept of a distinctive identity of the Manipuri people was promoted by some young educated elites who were greatly influenced by the Indian national liberation movement. They strongly opposed the colonial and feudal system of administration. Their only dream was to establish a new system of administration and political concept based on democratic principle. At the same time they also tried to remove all sorts of social evils which were considered as an obstacle towards the establishment of social evils which were considered as an obstacle towards the establishment of social equilibrium among the different groups of people of Manipur.

The year 1938 was a great landmark in the history of the political parties of Manipur. It marked the beginning of the existence of political parties in the state. The birth of '*Nikhil Manipur Mahasabha*' as a political party with a basic objective for the 'establishment of a responsible government' in mNipur may be considered as a direct blow of the existence of the colonial and feudal system of administration in the state. Under the banner of this party, the people, who strongly believed in the democratic principles, have launched different types of political actions for the fulfilment of their demands like the 'establishment of responsible government' in Manipur and amalgamation of the administration of hills and plain etc. The demand for the establishment of a legislature of unilateral system with a hundred legislators of whom not less than 80 would be nominated by the Maharaja was a big contribution of this political party to the people of Manipur. These political parties were established in the pre-merger period of Manipur. The establishment of these political parties with political and social objectives has, undoubtedly laid a very good foundation for the emergence of other political parties with a new political concept based on social and economic reality.

Just after the merger of Manipur into India in the year 1949 the people of Manipur again witnessed political activities of different political organizations. The establishment of *Praja Socialist Party (PSP), Nationalist Socialist Democratic Party (NSDP), Kuki National Assembly (KNA), Manipur People Party (MPP), Kanglei League, Manipur Hill Union (MHU),* etc. have produced a new political outlook among the people of Manipur. With the growth of these state based political organizations, the idea of regionalism within the framework of the national political mainstream also gradually emerged in the minds of the people. The assertion of local interest or regional political identity particularly in the context of Manipur was mainly due to the birth of these political organizations. Therefore the establishment of the Federal

Party of Manipur may be taken as a step towards the reassertion for the promotion of the political identity of Manipur within the framework of the national political arena.

Federal Party of Manipur was established as a state level political organization on the foundation of some historical facts. It was an outcome of a series of informal discussions and debates of some prominent academicians and social workers of the state. The focal point of their debate and discussion was based on certain key issues of political, social, economic and cultural conditions of the state which was developed just after the merger of Manipur into India in the year 1949. While discussing the overall issues of the state they also made an intensive critical study of the integrity, sincerity and political wisdom of the national level political parties particularly in their relationship with the political situation of Manipur. Apart from this they also studied very carefully the political concept and principle of some regional political organizations. After having a close observation of the political attitude of these existing political parties they came to a conclusion that in exercising their political wisdom in the state they had little degree of sincerity and honesty in their approach. Therefore they were not able to understand fully the feeling of the people of Manipur. On the basis of this conclusion they were of the view that the existing undesirable political situation in the state was the outcome of the relationship between the national political parties and common people.

Manipur was integrated into India through a rough political weather. As a result of this, a serious debate is going on among the academicians and social activists on the nature and response of the common people on the merger issue and the political motive of the leaders of the Congress Party of both the 'State' and the 'Centre'. But one point was very clear in the mind of the people particularly the younger generation that the merger of Manipur into India was not on the line of the policy and principle of transparency. Therefore, they expressed their resentment to the blunder committed by the Maharaja of Manipur. The Indian Independence Act 1947 empowered the princely states of India either to join India or Pakistan or to become an independent state. But the Maharaja of Manipur did not opt for an independent Manipur. Instead of this he signed the *'Stand Still Agreement'* on the 11th August 1947 by which Manipur accepted the Indian suzerainty in respect of some key affairs like, 'Foreign Affairs, Finance, Communication, Defense', etc., The Maharaja also signed the Instrument of Accession Act on the same date. So, the signing of these two treaty documents produced a confusion in the political status of Manipur. Some writers made an attempt to project the political status of Manipur from 1947 to 1949 i.e. pre-merger period, as that of an independent state. This matter is still a subject of serious debate and further observations and interpretations may be required. Then on the 21st September 1949 the Maharaja of Manipur signed the merger agreement and on the 15th October Manipur was officially merged into India. A general feeling existed in the mind of the common people that the Maharaja of Manipur was compelled under duress to sign the 'Merger Agreement'. This is of one of the most important factor for the growth of unhappiness among the people particularly towards the Government of India. Indeed, if we go a bit deeper into detail on the whole political drama which was going on in Manipur and the activities and policies of the leaders of the Indian government, we can come to a safe conclusion that the Maharaja of Manipur might have been compelled to sign the merger agreement due to a serious psychological torture inflicted on him by the Indian political leadership. Thus one silly mistake on the political decision of the government of Manipur or the ignorance of the ruler of the state had brought a drastic negative change to the future political status of Manipur.

The elements of the pro-merger group had strongly

advocated that the integration of Manipur into India would bring peace and development in the state. But when it comes to reality things began to change beyond expectation and desire. This stage was the most pitiable political position of Manipur. Even the leaders of the pro-merger elements was also quite taken aback to see the new political development. Instead of giving the equal political status with the other states of India, the central government abolished all the democratic institutions which were established under the Manipur State Constitution Act 1947 and entire responsibility of the administration was put under the care of a single bureaucratic officer. The refusal of the Government of India to establish the responsible government in Manipur was based mainly on the pretext of the lack of democratic experience. From the evidence it can be observed that their view was highly politically motivated because the people of Manipur had more political experience then the people of the rest of India. Then on the 22nd January 1950 the Government of India by an official declaration, granted Manipur the political status of a 'Part C' state under the Constitution of India. After twenty three years of central rule Manipur was granted 'Statehood' in 1972. That too happened after having witnessed a series of political agitations, which caused bitterness and mutual mistrust. The people, after getting the experience of unfair deal from of the Government of India, felt that the central leaders neglected them and gradually their sense of dissatisfaction and alienation were expressed in different forms.

The post-merger economic condition in Manipur was not to the satisfaction and desire of the people. After having a close observation of the economic trend in this state from the time of the integration the general people began to feel that Manipur had become a victim of neo colonialism. Though it is not required to go into detail it can be recalled that the present trend of economic growth in this state was the outcome of the removal of restriction imposed on the non-Manipuri people on the 18th November 1950. If the merits and demerits of this system are to be analysed it can be suggested that it rendered a great help to the people of Manipur in general in the process of the protection of local people from all possible aspects of the economic exploitation from the capitalist elements of other areas. But just after the removal of this system the traders from outside the state began to enter into Manipur without any restriction and started to play a dominating role in the economic life of the state. To see these undesirable economic conditions of the state and the role played by the outside traders, the members of the 'Assembly Demand Co-ordination Committee' submitted a memorandum to the President of India in which they regarded the new administrative policy of the Central Government as a systematic practice for 'gradual-de-Manipurization'. These deteriorating economic positions of the Manipuri people were further intensified by the rampart corruption in the administration led by a highly irresponsible political leadership and manned by a non-committed bureaucracy. They were not ready to take any type of responsibility either for the development of the state or to take care of the feeling, aspiration and interest of the common people of Manipur. The developmental funds have not reached to the needy persons of urban, rural and tribal areas. They were not prepared to provide the scope for the promotion of a self-generating economy. There was no industry and no factory which could provide job facilities to the educated youth. The cheap money created by the ill regulated spending of the Government promoted a market consumerism. Instead of self-sufficiency in her economic position Manipur had become dependent heavily to the Central Government. Practically, the production level was very much far below the consumption requirements. All the state enterprises and undertakings have failed. The people in the Government also were not prepared to extend all type of possible help to promote the private enterprises. Rather they tried to kill the efforts of private enterprises in collusion with the people from outside Manipur. As a result of this the opportunity for giving employment to the educated youth was completely stopped. There was no employment generating enterprises or undertakings. The state Government did not take any keen interest in the development of the state. They were not able to do anything for the welfare of the people and gradually they were acting as a salary giving agency only. There was no justice in the process of getting job and it depends entirely to the system of the highest bidder. All the financial institutions were not able to make any effective investment either for one reason or other. As a result of this, Manipur was under a situation of complete economic stagnancy. There was no capital investment. On the other hand the capital was fleeing from Manipur. Practically the Manipur State was not able to get much benefit under the New Economic Policy of the Government of India. In fact there was a complete financial bankruptcy in the state of Manipur. The political leadership and bureaucracy remained as a silent spectator as if nothing was happening in the state.

In the midst of this economic condition the state again witnessed a new social development, i.e. exploitation of poor by the rich and powerful groups. The gap between the haves and have-nots had widened beyond reparable stage. A new social class emerged in the state. This social class, i.e. neo-rich which was the creation of the new economic condition has controlled the Government and economy of Manipur. Under this non-economic trend and financial management the rural and tribal peasantry became a deprive group of the society. The helpless urban middle class people also began to depend for their existence on this new economic system. In the meantime a large scale influx of foreigners and the people from the other parts of the country have aggravated the economic situation of the state. The large scale influx of uncheck immigrants had caused constraints on land, natural resources, trade and commerce. Apart from this it also caused a serious demographic imbalances and social tensions. This new changes became a serious concerned among the people. They thought that this new development was a threatening call for the loss of their identity. Indeed, the new economic trend that was developed just after integration had produced a serious social impact in the state. Due to the lack of facilities of income generating unit and absence of the provision for development, Manipur became an important market place for the finished products of the big industries of the other parts of the country. No doubt the central government gave certain amount of money annually to the state government mainly for developmental purposes. But the present system of financial administration in state did not make any positive room for developmental works. Therefore the money which they have given to the state for developmental purpose again went back to the centre. This system of policy was nothing but to change the money from right hand to left and vice versa without any concrete objective. The ultimate result was that the status of the people of Manipur was changed from the position of master to the level of beggars. Under this economic position the life of the people of Manipur was at the mercy of the central government of India. Such type of system was the practice of neo-colonialism. The coming of a large quantity of industrial products from the mainland India finally gave a good shape for a complete destruction of the whole economy of the Manipur state. From this economic condition many people of the state began to feel that the people of Manipur became a victim of the internal colonialism.

The frightful increase of the number of educated unemployment people was also an immediate outcome of the new economic policy. Since there was no employment generating enterprises or understanding, the educated youths had no employment opportunities. The state Government was not able to provide any type of self-generating employment opportunities. Rather they became purely a salary-giving agency. The apprehension of the common people was that under this economic condition Manipur would be strangled to death economically.

Apart from these political and economic conditions the people of Manipur had also witnessed a series of violent type of separatist movement which vehemently emphasized for the establishment of a distinctive political identity of the Manipuris outside the political boundary of the Indian Union. The outbreak of such type of revolutionary movement may be treated as an immediate outcome of the deteriorating political and economic conditions in the state and a kind of expression of dissatisfaction to the integrity and sincerity of the leaders of Indian Government, which was developed since the integration of the state into India. On the other hand it also had greatly weakened the state and created a cause for a social tension among the ethnic groups of people. This trend of social tension was continuing for about two decades and it costs the life of the common people. However the state machinery did not make any serious attempt to protect the life and property of the common people. Rather in the name of maintaining the law and order situation they actively indulged in the act of state terrorism. Here lies a big question on the sincerity, integrity and motive of the people who were in the driver's seat of the administration. State terrorism is not the direct answer to the solution of the problem. Because of the lack of sincerity and unclear motive of the law enforcing mechanism like the military, para-military and police Manipur was made a police state. On the other hand the ruling group of the state which was constituted mostly by the opportunist politicians and selfish bureaucrats was not able to perform their duties effectively because in every inch of their work they were highly influenced by their selfish and opportunistic mentality. Thus due to the lack of political will and vision the people in the ruling clique was not able to see the real situation the same time they were not able to protect the life and property of the people of the state. Finally it led to the outbreak of serious violation in the basic human rights of the people of Manipur.

To see this highly undesirable new political and economic situation which was witnessed after the integration, the people began to question the sincerity and wisdom of the national and regional level political parties in the state. One of the important questions was whether what type of role they have played so far to protect and maintain the historical identity of the people of the state from the clutches of the new economic and administrative policy. It is quiet obvious that just after the merger of Manipur into India and being a democratic state the whole responsibilities of the people and state was in the hand of political parties. It is also convinced that they were not able to act effectively to safeguard the interest of the people. In that case what was the most important reason which compelled them not to take any political decision in the interest of the people of Manipur? In this respect two issues can be discussed first they are not able to take any political steps to the desire of the people because of the lack of political wisdom of the leadership of political parties. Secondly they were compelled not to act freely by their ideological principles.

While analyzing these problems it became an imperative to reopen the chapters of the political history of Manipur which was developed from the merger of the state. In this respect the role played by the national level political parties at the time of the crucial political juncture of the state of Manipur may be recalled. Among the national level political parties the role of the Congress Party was the most important. It is a well-known fact that the Congress Party was the torchbearer of the pro-merger elements of the people of Manipur. Their strong view was that if Manipur merged into India there would be a significant development in all aspects of the life of the state and it would bring welfare of the masses. Most of the educated people of that time were in favour of the integration. Taking the opportunity of the political environment of the given situation of that period the Manipur State Congress party in collusion with the Congress leaders of India brought Manipur state as a political unit of the Indian Union. However, its subsequent result was not to the expectation of the people of the state. Even the members of the State Congress party were not happy at the new political development. But they were not able to do anything on the tune of the desire of the people, as they were not able to go out beyond the boundary of the party principle. Their only duty was to act on the dictation of the Central leaders. Due to this limited position they were not able to represent the feelings of the desire of the people of Manipur. Another political parties of national level stature were Praja Socialist Parties and Samjukta Socialist Party. The local leaders of these parties also were not able to go against the interest of the outlook of other central leaders. Rather these parties made one step forward on the line of the Indianization principle. It was mainly from their demand that the government of Manipur have abolished all rules of restriction given to the non-Manipuri people. The removal of this system gave a good opportunity to the non-Manipuri people to enter into Manipur without any restrictions. They justified their demand on the ground that since Manipur was part of India there should not be any type of restriction to the other people of India while entering into Manipur. Free movement of people inside the boundary of India should be encouraged. The argument of the Socialist Party was also endorsed by the Congress Party. The removal of this system had rendered a great contribution in the process of the deteriorating economic position of Manipur. After the removal of this system many traders and businessmen from outside had entered into Manipur freely and started their business. The outbreak of a serious economic exploitation was the immediate outcome of this view policy. So far their political attitude to Manipur was concerned the Socialist Party as a main opposition political party of the state had severely criticized the Congress Party for their deliberate refusal to grant a responsible government in this state. But because of their ideological and constitutional bindings the members of the Socialist Party in Manipur was also not able to speak much for a distinctive political identity of the state. The same trend was also in the case of the Communist Party of India. No doubt Manipur had an experience of left movement under the leadership of Hijam Irabot Singh in which they strongly advocated for the welfare of the peasantry in the state. They also strongly demanded for the abolition of feudal system of administration and existing class discrimination in the society. In addition to this Hijam Irabot Singh also emphasized to promote and foster the distinctive features of the identity of the people of Manipur. But in later years the political motive of the new leadership of Communist Party was quite contradictory to Irabot and their approach was not in the same political line of their one time leader. Rather their mind and political culture also were influenced by the political principles of their parent organisation. Therefore, like other national parties they also were not able to give much thought for a distinctive identity of Manipuri people.

Apart from the political objectives and characters of the various national level political parties Manipur also had enjoyed a very good experience of other local or state level political parties. Starting from the *Nikhil Manipuri Mahasabha*, a local party of pre-independence period the people had witnessed the political activities of *Praja Sanmeloni, Praja Sangha, Krishak Sabha, Praja Mandol, Praja Shanti, Manipur National Union, Nationalist Socialist Democratic Party (NSDP)*, and *Manipur People's Party (MPP)* etc. In addition to this there were some local political parties which were based mainly on the ethnic line in the hill area like, *Kuki National Assembly (KNA)*, Paite Union etc. Among them the most important political party is *Manipur People's Party*. The main ideological foundation of this party is for the welfare and promotion of a distinctive identity of the state. On the basis of this ideological plank even the people of Manipur had voted this party to power. But this party, though they had enjoyed the confidence of the people, was not able to come up to the expectation of the people so far as the unity move of all the different ethnic groups of people of Manipur was concerned. Indeed, from the experience of their long existence as a political party, it can be observed that though they were able to lead the people in the valley area they were not able to penetrate into the hill areas very successfully. It seems that there were some kinds of gap of understanding, so far the aspect of political agendas between the leadership of the party and hill people. Though it is very difficult to give a clear picture of the reason of the gap of understanding it was quite evident from their nature that the tribal people had some reservation to the political approach of this regional party. As a result of this the Manipur People's Party, in spite of their best possible attempt, could not penetrate into the interior hill areas.

After having a good experience of the political nature of both national and state level political parties and to see the undesirable political development in the state which caused a good reason for instability in the natural identity of the people and state, a large section of the people , who strongly believed in the democratic process of change began to look for a better alternative political platform which can represent the feeling of the masses of both hills and plains. As a first step they started to make a close observation about the inner feeling of the masses as they thought that the strength of their political activities would come out from them.

Then they also analysed the history of the political developments in the state from the time of the integration and its impact. At the same time they also discussed the position of Manipur in the 'Indian Federation'. The Indian Constitution is very clear on the question of federation. The Constitution mentioned that "India is a Union of

States" It provides a political structure which according to Dr. B.R. Ambedkar is federal in normal time and unitary in extra-ordinary situation. In regard to the necessity of federal polity A.C. Kapur said "The constitution makers of independent India were in no doubt that a large new state, faced with the problem of establishing a central authority strong enough to govern a vast area inhabited by millions of people with different historical and linguistic backgrounds and interests, must inevitably be some form of federal structure. With the integration of princely states, the formation of federation had become a fait accompli".[1]

As we have mentioned above the undesirable and critical relationship between Manipur and the Government of India. Indeed to keep Manipur for 23 years under central rule was nothing but to violate the basic principle of Indian Constitution by the law enforcing agencies of the Central Government and breach of the basic fundamental right of the people of Manipur. To grant statehood in 1972 after several political agitations did not make any positive healthy atmosphere in the people to people relationship. Because during this long period of time people had witnessed a lot of undesirable and unexpected political scene which caused for the development of bitterness and mistrust mindset among the people particularly the younger generation group. Finally it led for the creation of a serious gap of understanding between the people of Manipur and Government of India. The people of Manipur had an impression that the central leaders had deliberately neglected the people of the state for reasons not known to them and a sense of dissatisfaction was developed to the attitude of the Government of India. Such type of attitude was regarded by the people as a policy of colonialism under the garb of democratic fineness'.[2] After having an experience of the nature of deliberate ignorance the people began to express their dissatisfaction and alienation in different forms.

Such type of development in the relationship between

the Central Government and state of Manipur was not a healthy political atmosphere under the democratic norms. Therefore the people who were the strong preacher for the growth of the value of parliamentary democracy had expressed their desire to re-examine and redefine the relation between the centre and the state. There was an impression among the political and social observers in the state that the problem of political, economic and psychological nature of Manipur would be able to resolve if the principle of federalism as provided in the Indian constitution were fully implemented. Apart from this the problem of the plural society is also another important feature which sometimes creates problem in the process of democratic functioning. It is believed that in order to operate the democratic principles successfully a cohesive society based on social justice and social harmony with full protection of the cultural identity of the people should be established. The concept of unity in diversity in social and cultural life should be encouraged because such a society will fulfil the social aspiration of various communities. So, it is said that the social chaos and social fissures which is now a problem in Manipur can be resolved and eradicated by a political system, based on ethnic pluralism and social federalism.[3]

In addition to this the people of Manipur also faced a serious problem of economic stagnancy which was created by the corrupt administration and unprincipled political leadership. As already been mentioned above the people of Manipur, particularly of the younger generation group, felt that 'Manipur is the victim of neo-colonialism' and Manipur's economy was at the mercy of the 'Capitalist economic system of mainland India'. This economic crisis in Manipur was caused by the rampant corruption in the administration led by a highly irresponsible political leadership and manned by a non-committed bureaucracy.[4] While this was the situation in the state the people who witnessed a serious problem of instability due to the outbreaks of revolutionary movements. Such type of development had greatly weakened the state and caused social tensions. On the other hand in the name of maintaining law and order situation the law enforcing machineries namely military, para-military and police forces are choking the state and they have made Manipur a police state.[5] To see all these undesirable and unprecedented developments, it is observed that "the state as an 'institution' has declined in Manipur, if it has yet to wither away in the Marxian way".[6]

Finally it has come to a safe conclusion that the only possible way to pull out Manipur from the present political and social instability was to bring a positive drastic radical change in every life of the people of the state. In this respect a group of political activists and intellectuals felt that there are only two possible ways. One was violent type of political movement and another was non-violent type of political movement. But most of them were the strong believers in the democratic process. Therefore they opted for a non-violent political movement which is based on the basic principles of democratic process. They are of the view that since the Indian Government is enjoying the democratic principle of parliamentary form of government, a vision for a radical change of the Manipur state would be possible only through the ballot war. In this connection they also believed that the problem of Manipur could be highlighted very successfully through a platform of a political party which has a capacity to represent the feeling of the people. But they are not in favour of existing national and local parties. They thought that since they had an experience of the terrible failure on their basic duty it was not advisable to test them again. Therefore they preferred for a new party with a clear-cut ideology and basic political agendas. They also believed that regional party would serve the local interest better than other national parties.

It is said that the emergence of regional political parties in Indian polity is a "national expression of the democratic will of the people for extension of autonomy based on federalist sentiments under the constitution".[7] The expression of the democratic will of the people on the issue of the local interest is an outcome of the dialectical response to the hegemonic centralism of the government of India. It is a fact that the national level political parties who are now playing the major role in Indian policies and who controlled the government are the representatives of the capitalistic and chauvinistic vested interest of the Indian upper castes and classes. [8] Apart from the political issues the disparity in the level of economic development is also another strong factor for the growth of regionalism in the minds of the people of the state. It is said that the greatest endogenous factor is the strong urge of the people to preserve their cultural, linguistic and ethnic identity. [9] So those regional issues and aspiration are expressed through the political movements.

On the basis of this understanding and keeping in view of the immediate need for a democratic political change they have decided to form a new political platform which could represent all the feelings and aspirations of the people of Manipur. It is a fact that "a political party in a democracy is an instrument of social change". They were also of the view that this new proposed political party would be formed on the federal principle which aims at restructuring the relationship between the Federal Government and state. They also believed that this party would delivered the best alternative to redeem the people of Manipur from the present mess and built up a bright future.

REFERENCES

1. Kapur, A.C. 1985. *Constitutional History of India.* New Delhi: S. Chand and Co. Ltd. p. 406.
2. *Federal Party of Manipur (The Basic Issue).* 1993. p. 1.
3. Ibid. pp. 3-4.
4. Ibid. p. 6.

5. Ibid. p. 6.
6. Kamei, Gangmumei. 1993. Emergence of Regionalism in North East India. Speech delivered at 3rd Conference of the Commonwealth Parliamentary Association, N.E. Region held at Imphal. p. 11.
7. Ibid.
8. Ibid. p. 13.

CHAPTER TWO

PARTURITION

Just after the completion of the formation of ideological framework those political and social activists have prepared to translate their political objective into action for peaceful democratic change in the state. Accordingly a public meeting was convened by those groups of people on 21st October 1993 at 10:00 a.m. at Majorkhul Community Hall. The main objective of the meeting was to invite the opinion of the masses particularly the people who were the strong believer in democratic values and its norms and social workers of the state to give their opinion and suggestion in regard to the immediate need for the establishment of a new political platform through which the desire and aspiration of the people could be expressed without any exception. The public meeting was convened at the initiative of a group of conveners. Their names were (1) Dr. N. Joykumar Singh (2) Dr. M. Jitendra Singh (3) Dr. Vanlalnghak (4) Seipu Sitlhou and (5) Ashinpu Gangmei.[1] It was a well attended meeting. Some prominent personalities of Manipur were also present and actively participated in the deliberations. This public meeting was presided over by Shri Naorem Birendrakumar Singh, a well-known political activist, a noted journalist of the state and editor of 'Paojel' a Manipuri daily newspaper.

In order to have a more convenient atmosphere in the process of discussion and deliberation the organizers have placed five basic issues. The 'Basic Issues' circulated by the organizers were (a) Manipur in the Indian Federation, (b) Ethnic pluralism and social federalism, (c) Economic stagnancy, (d) Insurgencies and revolution: Need for a dialogue and (e) Autonomy for Manipur.

(a) Manipur in the Indian Federation:

In regard to the question of the political status of Manipur in the Indian Federation, the basic issue paper, after giving a detail historical analysis of how the state had integrated into the political boundary of the Indian Union and its subsequent political developments, had categorically come to a conclusion that the merger of Manipur into India was not in a happy and harmonious way. At the same time though Manipur got statehood she was not able to get a fair deal from the India Government.[2] Therefore, the approach paper made a proposal to re-examine and re-define the relationship between the state and the Union of Indian Republic. It is also felt that the key problems of Manipur could be solved only with the by implementation of the principles of federation which is clearly provided in the Indian constitution. The paper also gave a critical observation about the nature of Indian federation. It pointed out that since federation implies division of powers and functions of the government between 'Federal Union' and 'Federating states', the interest of small state should be well protected. In this regard the paper strongly asserted that "The Indian polity and Indian nationhood with its pluralistic foundation are to be interpreted to maintain the Indian unity and integrity by protecting and accommodating the interest and aspirations of the minorities and of the smaller states like Manipur". [3] It further pointed out that over centralization of power in the union government have greatly weakened the position of the states particularly the minority and smaller states. Therefore, it is felt necessary to re-examine the center and state relationship so that the small groups and their states would be made to feel secure and proud to be the members of the 'Indian Republic and Nation'. In this connection the approach paper raised a basic point for an elaborate discussion on the center and state relationship. It strongly emphasized that there should be decentralization of the power. But this does not mean that the administrative position of the Central Government should be weakened. The positive argument, which was highlighted in the approach paper, was that by application of federal principles both the Federal Government and Manipur would gain in regulating their relationship. Rather Manipur state would be able to get an opportunity to harmonize the various sections of her population in their intra-state relationship.[4] On the basis of these observation and in order to review the present polity of India, a strong political slogan i.e. 'Federalism is the need of the hour ', was placed as a banner or a big stride of a political movement.

(b) Ethnic pluralism and social federalism:

It is also true that ethnic problem always influenced the body politic of every state and its society. The political stability of any given state is possible only when there is a less ethnic problem. India is a plural society and every different ethnic group of people has the privilege to enjoy their distinctive linguistic, religions and cultural affiliations. The same trend is also in the case of Manipur. The three major ethnic groups in Manipur are Meitei, Naga and Kukis. The small groups like Meitei Pangal (Muslim) and non-Manipuri etc. has been living together with other ethnic communities. Thus they represent a picture of ethnic pluralism with their homogeneity and heterogeneity. However it is felt that the social harmony among the different ethnic group would be possible only when there are mutual respect and honour among them. It is proposed that every ethnic community, whatever the size of the number of people may be, should have the privilege to protect foster and preserve their national identity. The approach paper proposed that a cohesive society based on social justice and social harmony with full protection of the cultural identity of people should be built up[5] so that it would greatly help in the process of the strengthening of political stability in the state. If this process is to be implemented definitely it would fulfill the social aspiration of the various communities. With these observations the approach paper proposed a new idea for discussion that in order to have a healthy political atmosphere a new political system should be initiated based on ethnic pluralism and social federalism. It is also believed that the present social chaos and social fissures could be resolved and eradicated only by this political system and at the same time it would be able to check the possibility of the emergence of dangerous 'Social Darwinism'.

(c) Economic stagnancy:

Indeed, the character of the present political development in a particular state is highly influenced by the nature of the economy. The economy is the backbone for the stability and strengthening of the body politic of any nation. In this respect the approach paper gave a highly scientific analysis about the economic position of Manipur and her relationship with other financial agencies of 'Central Government'. It has been already mentioned in the previous chapter about the stage of complete stagnancy of the economic position of Manipur. It was the outcome of the nature of administration created by the highly irresponsible political leadership with the help of non-committed bureaucracy. It is also true that just after integration the Government of India, as a part of their administrative responsibility, invested money in Manipur through massive development plans. But under the present system of administration the invested money, which was sent as a developmental fund, have not reached to the needy people, the urban poor, the rural and tribal peasantry.[6] On the other hand the cheap money created by the ill regulated spending of the government has promoted market consumerism. So, this ill regulated economic system has brought no expected development in the field of industry and agriculture. The dream of the self-sufficiency, which was enjoyed by the people of Manipur before integration, was completely shattered. So far the financial matter is concerned Manipur has become heavily dependent on the Central Government. It is also pointed out that all the state enterprises and undertaking have failed and 'what is going on is an uncontrolled state capitalism'. [7] It is further mentioned that the quantity production was far below the consumption requirements, the per capita income of Manipur was extremely low at the present inflationary rate, there was a frightful increase in educated unemployment and there was no employment generating enterprises or undertakings. To get job also was difficult and it was possible only to the highest bidders. The capital was fleeing from Manipur and the financial institutions also were not able to make an effective investment. With these observations the approach paper concluded that under this financial position Manipur was under complete economic stagnancy and if this situation was to be continued further Manipur would be strangled to death economically.

It was also pointed out that this new economic system of India has laid a basic foundation for the exploitation of poor by the rich and powerful section of the society. A kind social situation, which was the creation of new economic system, also emerged in the state of Manipur. The neo-rich class has merged and they have controlled the government and economy of Manipur. The urban middle class has heavily depended on this new social and economic group. On the other hand the rural and tribal peasantry becomes a deprived section in the society. When this was the situation Manipur again faced a serious economic problem due to the large-scale influx of foreign national from her neighbouring area. Apart from the demographic imbalance the uncheck influx of foreigners had caused constraints on land, natural resources, trade and commerce. Therefore there was a serious apprehension among the thinkers that these accumulated problems might give a serious threat to the national identity of the Manipuri people and to the conditions of the future economy of Manipur.

(d) Insurgencies and revolution:

On the question of insurgencies and revolutions it is also mentioned that the outbreak of these movements were directly or indirectly related with the growth of political and new economic development. Therefore it was also suggested that though it had produced a social tension among the people, it could be solved either by a natural course or through conscious efforts. It is true that no political problem is insoluble. However to terrorise the people was not the solution of the problem. It is also observed that the basic duty of the state is to protect the lives and property of the citizen. Whereas in the case of Manipur, opportunist politicians and selfish bureaucrats had compelled the state not to perform its duty. So the whole state machinery was totally failed in their basic duty. The biggest tragedy on their part, as pointed out in the approach paper, was that, these politicians and ruling cliques had neither the moral courage nor the vision to deal with the revolutionary situation in the state. In addition to this the outbreak of frequent ethnic clash among the tribal people had further deteriorated the law and order situation of the state. On the foundation of this existing situation it is observed that since these revolutionary organizations had launched the movement with a basic political social and economic objective which cannot be dealt with from the framework of Indian Constitution. It is necessary to initiate dialogue between the Federal Government and revolutionary group. It was felt that to have a dialogue with them would be able to pull out Manipur from this grim situation as well as from the clutches of the incompetent and selfish government. It was further proposed that the dialogue between the Federal Government and revolutionaries should be made through the service of some dedicated peacemakers.

(e) Autonomy for Manipur

As has already been discussed about the nature of integration of Manipur into India and its subsequent political development particularly in the context of Center and State relationship. From these historical facts it is quite evident that it was not a happy union and the subsequent relationship was also not to the desire and expectation of the people of Manipur. Under this existing constitutional and political system Manipur has been depending on the Federal Government for its own survival. The present existing relationship Manipur did not provide adequate autonomy to Manipur to deal with the complex socio-economic and political problems confronting the state. Every decision for the future of Manipur was always taken by the political leadership of Federal Government and the state government was just dovetail in their decision. It is also felt that every state in the Indian republic should have enough autonomy so that the people would be able to participate in the decision making concerning their future.

In the context of Manipur a proposal was made for a large scale debate on the question whether Manipur State should be restored to the status of internal autonomy under the Manipur State Constitution merger Act 1947 i,e. the administrative position which were in practiced from 1947 till the merger of the state into India and the terms of the Stand Still Agreement and Instrument of Accession between Manipur and the Indian Government signed on August 11, 1947 should be the basis of Manipur's autonomy and her relationship with the Federal Government of India".[8] It is also said that this proposed idea was not meant to return to monarchy. The concept of feudalism and feudal system of administration was an outdated and rejected principle particularly in the context of Manipur. It is further proposed that the principle of autonomy should not be confined only to the center. It should be extended at the districts and village levels including the hill areas. In the context of Center and State relationship and granting of maximum autonomy to the state, the approach paper also mentioned the relevancy of the recommendation of 'Sarkaria Commission'.

With this conceptual framework and broad observations the deliberation of the public meeting was initiated by the president. Each and every person who attended the meeting fully participated in the discussion. This was also an unanimous view among the participants that only a new local based political party alone would serve the regional and local interest better than other national political parties. They also opinioned that the state of Manipur and people as well required a regional based political party who possessed a high degree of political will having a strong commitment and determination to protect and promote the interest of the people. The members also felt that such type of political party alone would be able to solve the problems of Manipur. At the same time they also endorsed the critical observations of 'Basic Issue' placed for further discussion on the state of relationship between Federal Government and Manipur State. It was also an unanimous view of all the participants that in order to promote and protect the interest of the state a strong demand should be initiated for the restructuring of relation between Federal Government and Manipur State. Thus after having a detail discussions and deliberations all the members had unanimously agreed to establish a new political party with the following broad objectives: They were:-

(i) To ensure freedom, democracy and human rights to the people of Manipur as enshrined in Indian Constitution;

(ii) To build up a new Social Order based on social and economic justice, social harmony and cultural pluralism;

(iii) To restructure the relationship between Manipur and the Federal Government of India on the federal principles and historical rights of Manipur based on the pre-merger political states.

(iv) To promote and preserve the unity and common identity of Manipur within the canvass of ethnic pluralism and social federalism;

(v) To provide autonomy in administration at the district and village levels both in the hill and valley of Manipur;

(vi) To preserve and promote the common cultural heritage of the people of Manipur with proper respect for and protection of the ethnic and cultural ethos and religious beliefs of the different section of the population;

(vii) To build up an economic system with the following features:

(a) Economic planning to promote development with social justice;

(b) Equitable economic development of various sections and regions of the state, free from exploitation of one group/class by the other.

(c) Proper utilization of and social control over the natural resources access to which shall properly regulated by the state;

(d) Encouragement of private enterprises for development.

(e) Involvement of foreign capital in the development plans of the state.

(viii) To preserve the natural balance in the ecology and environment of the state and prevent pollution and other evil effects of development projects on the life of the people.

(ix) To take up steps for the preventions of the alienation of land to the non-indigenous immigrants;

(x) To frame suitable land laws for the hill areas of Manipur keeping in view the need for preparation of record of rights for tribal land owners and flow of institutional finance for tribal development;

(xi) To take up measures for the upliftment of the position

and states of woman in respect of their role in the social economic and political life of the state;

(xii) To establish fraternal contact with regional portion of country especially for those of the northeastern states and take up common steps on the problems of common interests. It shall be fraternal relationship with those groups and organizations which believe in then federal base of the Indian polity.[9]

It is very interesting to note that all the participants in the public meeting had an impression in their mind that the idea of the formation of a new political party with these ideological frameworks would certainly lay a big foundation for a large scale revolutionary change in the social, political and economic life of the people of Manipur. Some members even expressed that the conceptual groundwork of this new proposal was so comprehensive that it covers almost all the aspects of the life of a human beings. With great enthusiasm all the members have actively participated in the process of long deliberation.

Thus after having a detail discussion about the political scenario in Manipur right from the beginning of the integration into India and the subsequent relationship between India and Manipur under the existing system of Center-State relationship and its impact on the social and economic life of the people in particular, this public meeting unanimously agreed to form a new political party based on the commitment of regional character and local interest. The resolution of the public meeting runs like this:–

1. RESOLUTION ON THE FORMATION OF FEDERAL PARTY OF MANIPUR

This **PUBLIC MEETING** of political leaders, social activists and community leaders representing all sections and regions of Manipur, after having discussed the political, economic, social and administrative structure and its relationship with the Government of India under the system over centralization of power with Union Government and inadequate autonomy for the state solemnly expresses:

ITS GREAT CONCERN over Manipur's current political, economic and social crisis and the failure of the state administrative machinery to cop with it;

THE NEED TO RESTRUCTURE THE relationship between Manipur and Government of India on the basis of federal principles which would ensure decentralization of power and autonomy to the state in administrative and financial matters;

THAT THE EXISTING political leadership and their parties have proved to be ineffective in solving the crisis in Manipur;

THAT THERE IS A NEED TO MOBILISE all the progressive secular and democratic forces under a common political forum to redeem Manipur from the present morass and build up a new Social Order in the state;

It is hereby solemnly resolved to form a regional political party under the name and style of **FEDERAL PARTY OF MANIPUR.** [10] (Extract of the Resolution)

After taking the formal resolution of the formation of a new political party, this meeting adopted another resolution to constitute a drafting committee to prepare the constitution of Federal Party of Manipur and all the members of the office bearers of the party was made the members of the committee. Along with this the steps for the registration of Federal Party of Manipur to the Election Committee of India was also prepared.

Just after the completion of the frameworks for the establishment of a political party the meeting began to take special attention for the election of the party leader and other office bearers. In the process of discussion all the participants expressed their desire to put the responsibility of leadership of the party to a person having the character of integrity, sincerity and honesty. They expressed this opinion after having a long experience of nature of the working of other political parties in Manipur. Keeping all the views particularly on the problems of social tensions and ethnic clash, majority of the participants was of the opinioned that the leadership of the party should be given to a person who possess all the quality to see the totality of the whole problem in the state and who can see both hill and plan people together. On the basis of this logical observation some expressed their desire to give the responsibility of leadership to Prof. Gangmumei Kamei from Majorkhul, Imphal. Then the meeting finally elected him as the first and founder president of Federal Party of Manipur.

Other members of the office bearers were:-

Vice Presidents	–	Shri Ng. Nimai Singh
		Dr. Lal Dena
		Shri M. Maringa
		Shri Kumar Singh
General Secretary	–	Shri S.H. Sheipu
		Dr.N.Joykumar Singh
		Dr. M. Jitendra Singh
		Dr. Van Lalnghak
Treasurer	–	Shri Khelen Singh
Secretary	–	Shri Asinpao Gangmei
		Shri KameshwarSingh

This meeting also authorized the president to constitute a Central Executive Committee of the party.

BACKGROUND OF LEADERS

Leadership is the most important aspect of every organization. It is true that the success and failure of any type organization is entirely in the hand of the leaders and the importance and credibility of the political parties are measured from the degree of the quality and maturity of the leaders of any particular party. In one sense the leadership is the best measuring rode or scale of every common people to judge the political maturity and credibility of the party. This is the basic issue in the process of the selection of leadership. The participants were very much particular about the leader and the office bearers who has to act as the custodian of the ideology and objective of the party. Finally the members, after having a close examination of their sincerity and integrity, have unanimously agreed to give the responsibilities for the running of the party to the fpllowing persons.

Prof. Gangmumei Kamei, who was elected by the 'Public Meeting' as the founder President of Federal Party of Manipur was a Professor in the Department of History, Manipur University and a celebrated academician not only in Manipur but also to other parts of North-Eastern region. As an academician he had written a number of research papers and books on various aspects of the history of Manipur. Through writing he was able to bring a new revolutionary change in the process of writing and interpretation particularly in the study of regional history. Apart from his professional credibility he was a man of dedicated social worker. He was also one of the founder leaders of 'Cultural Integration Conference', a social organization which strongly advocated for the unity and harmony among the various section of the people of Manipur. Through this organization he enjoyed a privilege to have a close contact with different section of people. This is a rare experience and additional quality that is supposed to posses by every leader. He was also a dreamer and has a very good quality of farsightedness. In every work he was very critical and always makes a sound judgment and right decision. Another important quality he had possessed was that he was a man of very accommodative nature. He was able to make friendship with any person whatever the age, caste; creed and colour might be. On top of this he had a wonderful vast experience about the ethos, culture, religion and history of the different ethnic community of Manipur. In addition to this he also had a good experience of the working of political organization in the state. From these vast professional knowledge, good political experience and art of social relationship he was considered by the members of the 'Public Meeting' as the right person to lead the party.

Shri Ng. Nimai Singh of Tabungkhok village in the Patsoi Assembly Constituency was a prominent leader of co-operative movement in Manipur.

Dr. Lal Dena from Churachandpur District was a prominent academician from Hmar community. He was a soft spoken man, who possessed the quality of sincerity and honesty. He was a social worker and actively involved in very social problems and issues of the tribal community in Manipur.

Shri M. Maringa a political activist. He was actively involved in many political activities of the state. He was also a worker and leader of MPP (Manipur People Party). He was also a Councilor of Imphal Municipal Board. Apart from his political involvement he was also a social activist. He was actively associated with many social and religious organizations of Zeliangrong Community.

Shri Kumar Singh was a social activist. Before he joined the party, he was in Government service. He was a man who possesses enough experience in the panchayat system of administration.

This four personalities, considering their political experience and social activities, were elected as the Vice Presidents of the newly formed party.

Shri S.H. Seipu was a social activist from the Sadar Hill area. Though he had little knowledge of the political activities, he was deeply involved in many social organizations. He was also a man of integrity and sincerity.

Dr. N. Joykumar Singh is a Professor of History in Manipur University. He is a social and political activist.

Right from the very young age he actively participated in various activities of political organizations and student movements. He was one of the founder members of Congress (I) in Manipur. He was very energetic and man of integrity. He was the most active spokesman of the new group of political thinkers.

Dr. M. Jitendra Singh was also a teacher in the History Department of Manipur University.

Dr.Van Valalnghak was a teacher in the Philosophy Department of Manipur University. He is a deeply religious man and a social activist. He is also involved in every social and religious activities particularly of Hmar Community. He is a man of integrity, honesty and sincerity. He is a very jolly man and very accomodative.

These members, considering from their educational and social backgrounds were elected as the General Secretaries of the party.

Thus with the formation of the body of the working committee the Federal Party of Manipur came into existence as state political party under the basic conceptual principle of federalism and autonomy.

REFERENCES

1. See Appendix No.1
2. 'Approach Paper' presented to and discussed at the public meeting at Imphal held on 21st October 1993-P.2
3. Ibid.
4. Ibid.
5. Ibid.
6. Ibid.
7. Ibid.
8. Ibid.
9. Reproduced from 'Approach Paper'
10. Reproduced from the proceedings of Public Meeting held on 21-10-93 at Community Hall, Majorkhul.

CHAPTER THREE

LEGITIMIZATION OF THE ORGANISATION

PRESENTATION OF DRAFT CONSTITUTION

As per Resolution No. 3 of the Public Meeting the president of the party had constituted a 'Constitutional Drafting Committee' with all the office bearers as members. And on the 9th November 1993 at1 p.m. a 'Special General Body' meeting of the party was convened at Majorkhul community hall to discuss and adopt the draft constitution of the party. It was a full pack session and all the formalities for deliberation was started formally with a welcome address given by Shri Ng. Nimai Singh the Vice President of the party.

In his opening remark, Prof. Gangmumei Kamei the president of the party said that Federal Party of Manipur is historically inevitable political party to redeem Manipur and forge a new and bright future. According to him "Federal Party is not a mere political party in a narrow sense of capturing power in a democratic set up. It is an instrument of social change. It is rather a movement expressing the long cherished desire and will of the people of the hills and valley of Manipur."[1] After giving a critical analysis of the political relationship between Manipur state and Government of India from year 1949 and by giving a detail explanation about the general feeling of the common masses he strongly asserted that the nature of the relationship between state and centre should be federal. On the basis of this conceptual idea he declared that the principle of "Federalism is the need of the hour". He further said, "a nation or a political community cannot survive alone on the basis of its relation with the external agencies or forces. They should posses internal strength and determined aspirations concretized into a political and social structure. Such a structure called the state is to carry out the task of nation building."[2] With this argument he had categorically emphasized that Federal Party of Manipur had a clear social and political vision for the future of Manipur. It was a very forceful presentation, which contents full of emotional appeals to the common people of Manipur. Indeed it laid a foundation for the rapid growth of Federal Party of Manipur, as a major political on in the political soil of Manipur.

He further said, "We want a united Manipur, where there is respect for the dignity of human individual, where there is equality of all men, where everybody is entitled to a descent living, where there is a social and economic justice, where the ethnic and social minority will lead a life of dignity and security, where there will be no oppression, no exploitation and where the poverty will be eradicated."[3] For a distinctive political identity of Manipur state he also strongly emphasized the immediate need to modify the nature of the Indian Union in Federal principles. He also encouraged the system of inner party democracy. He said, that Federal Party of Manipur had paid full respect to the constructive opinion of every section of the people of the state and it could be accommodated in the programme of action to be taken up by the party.

Just after giving a detail analytical objective he further said that "no constitution is complete and static. It has to grow and make changes to meet the political and social needs and aspirations of the people."[4] In the course of his deliberation he also make an appeal to the entire liberal, progressive, secularist and nationalist elements to join Federal Party of Manipur. Indeed it was a historic presidential address particularly for the members of the party. In his short speech he had successfully make an attempt to highlight the historical necessity of the establishment of Federal Party of Manipur as a new political party in the state.

NATURE OF PROPOSED DRAFT CONSTITUTION

The draft constitution was formally presented to the special session by Dr. N. Joykumar Singh ,the General Secretary and seconded by Dr. Vanlalnghak, the another General Secretary. The whole body of the proposed draft constitutions was constituted by 24 Articles. Though it was not a lengthy one the draft constitution has included all the requisite infrastructure and principles which was required by any political party.

The preamble of the proposed draft constitution runs like this:-

"Whereas having solemnly resolved to constitute a voluntary political organization of the people of Manipur and in order to: Ensure Freedom, Democracy and Human Right to the people of Manipur, Create a Social Ordered based on Social and Economic Justice, Welfare and Social Federalism. FEDERAL PARTY OF MANIPUR has been duly constituted and the constitution thereof has been adopted. Whereas required by law, Federal Party of Manipur do hereby declare that it shall bear "its true faith and allegiance to the Constitution of India as by law established and to the principles of Socialism, Secularism and Democracy and would uphold the sovereignty, unity and integrity of India."

The preamble of the constitution had clearly expressed its desire to build up a free and democratic society with an essence of overall development in the political, social, economic and cultural life of Manipur. In order to materialize these ideas the proposed constitution had emphasized certain objectives which covered almost all the aspects of the issue of the state. They also assured that the party would strive to achieve these objects. The objectives were: –

(i) To create a political and administrative structure in Manipur so as to facilitate the participation of all social and ethnic groups in the democratic process and nation building task in the state;

(ii) To restructure the relationship between the Union Government and the state of Manipur, based on federal principles and more autonomy for the state with full recognition of the historical prerogative of Manipur;

(iii) To promote economic development through planning, free from exploitation, with social control over the natural resources, encouragement of private enterprises, involvement of foreign capital and with full participation of the people in the process of planning and implementation of development process of the state;

(iv) To promote the common heritage of the various sections of Manipur's population and protect their cultural and ethnic identity and territorial integrity of the state;

(v) To promote the welfare of the tribal, minorities and other weaker sections of the society including women and physically handicapped persons;

(vi) To take up suitable steps for the attainment of the objectives by social and political action through democratic, constitutional and peaceful means;

(vii) To establish fraternal contact with others regional political parties of the country and with those groups and organizations which believe in the federal base of Indian polity.

The constitution also proposed two-tier system in the organizational structure i.e. State Level and District Level. It also proposed to have three important administrative branches of the party. They are (a) General Assembly (b) Central Committee and (c) Working Committee. The 'District Level' organizational structure proposed to have three branches i.e.; (a) District Committee (b) Kendra Committee and (c) Primary Unit.

In order to have an opportunity to understand the grievances and problems of different section of the society the draft constitution also proposed to open 'Frontal Organizations and Cells' of the party. Accordingly the idea for the opening of youth front, women front, peasant front, minority cell, scheduled casts and schedule tribes cell, teachers' cell, economic advisory cell, etc and physically handicapped cell was also proposed in the Article 5 (five). Article 6 (six) of the draft constitution also proposed for two types of membership of the party i.e. Primary and Active membership. A person of 18 years old was allowed to be the primary member of the party by paying an annual membership fee of Rs.1/– (one) and any primary member could be an active member after the completion of one year and he has to enroll 25 (twenty five) membership fee of Rs.10/– (ten) for active membership.

'General Body' was the supreme authority in the party's organizational structure. Article 7 (seven) of the draft constitution provides the nature of the constitution of this body. The election of the party president, delegation of relevant powers and duties to the central committee and working committee and amendment of the constitution of the party are the most remarkable powers of the 'General Body'. Article 8 (eight) provides the nature and composition of the 'Central Committee' and its power and functions. The most important duty of the body was to elect the Vice Presidents of the party and this committee would implement and carry out the policy and programme laid down by the General Assembly. Article 9 (nine) explained the nature of the composition of the members of the body working committee and Article 10 (ten) provides the power and function of the body. Thus from article 7 (seven) to article 10 (ten) are the most important parts in the whole body of the draft constitution. That these articles provide the nature of power and duties to these bodies, which are the most important anatomy of the whole body of the party as well as of the draft constitution.

The constitutions also mentioned about the nature of the composition, power and duties of the 'Districts', 'Kendras' and 'Primary Units' of the party. No doubt these bodies were the important feature of the proposed constitution and their basic duty was to play a major role with process of the expansion, and consolidation of the party. The detail information about the nature of these bodies was mentioned in the Article 11 (eleven) of the proposed constitution.

The power and function of the office functionary was mentioned very specifically in Article 13 (thirteen), 14 (fourteen), 15 (fifteen) and 16 (sixteen). Article 13 (thirteen) explained the position of the power of the President of the party. The constitution gives a supreme authoritative power to the president in the functioning of the party. Article 14 (fourteen) provides the power and duties of the vice President, Article 15 (fifteen) provides the duties of the General Secretaries and Joint Secretaries and Article 16 (sixteen) gave detail picture about the nature of the duty of treasure and auditor of the party.

Apart from this the proposed draft constitution also provides all the required features like nature of the meeting of the party and its quorum, election of party functionaries, nature of voting pattern, nature of disciplinary action to be taken against the party members etc. in different articles.

While presenting the draft constitution, Dr. N. Joykumar Singh gave a detail analysis about the existibg political and economic scenario in the state of Manipur. He also endorsed the view of the president that no constitution was complete and static. It has a big room to modify, amend and review. He also admitted that because of the demand of the situation the constitution of the party was prepared within a short possible time. With these few observations he also requested the members to discuss and adopt it formally.

After the presentation part was over the members of the 'Special General Body' began to give their observations and suggestions. However all of them agreed the spirit and also ideas expressed in the preamble of the constitution and welcomed the objectives given in the draft constitution. Thus after having a detail discussion all the members accepted the provisions of the proposed draft constitution and also agreed to adopt it as an official constitution of the party. With the adoption of party constitution Federal Party of Manipur began to launch its democratic revolutionary movement under the banner of her flag. The flag of the party had expressed different ideas. The orange colour, as explained in the constitution, represents, service, sacrifice and purity. 'Red Sun' represents source of life, energy, justice and victory. The General Assembly also proposed to request the Election Commission to allot one of the following symbols as mentioned below on the election symbol of the party. The proposed symbols were: - (1) Sangai, (2) A farmer holding a spade, (3) Two swords with a shield and (4) Pipal Tree.

One of the most dramatic and noteworthy events in the history of this party was that while the process of the adoption of constitution was about to complete the minds of the same of the members present perhaps were suddenly influenced by the believes of the traditional religious practices and they expressed their desire to take a vow at the sacred religious place of 'Kangla'. Accordingly all the members of the party took a long procession with banners and party flag to Kangla (inside the cantonment area) and reached exactly at 3:30 p.m. There was a 'Maibi' (an oracle) at Kangla. She made all the religious preparation to worship the deity. She said that it was the right time to worship the progenitor of Khuman clan. After the completion of religious ceremony the President gave a short speech and under his leadership all the members took a firm promise to work hard for the welfare of the people of Manipur and to protect and foster the distinctive political identity of the people of Manipur. Such type of spirit was a unique feature in the character of the founder members of the party.

PROVISIONAL REGISTRATION

Just after the completion of all the process of the adoption constitution the Federal Party of Manipur approached the Election Commission of India with a formal request to recognize them as a state based political party. On the 10th November 1993 a formal application in the official Performa was submitted to the Election Commission for registration as a political party under section 29 A of the Representation of the People Act, 1951. While submitting the application the party clearly stated that Federal Party of Manipur is based on 'National ideals, Democracy, Socialism, Secularism and Federalism, Regionalism and Social Federalism'. On the question of the policies, aims and objects the party categorically asserted that it would follow democratic constitutional and peaceful policy.[6] Apart from this the party also placed all the necessary information desired by the Commission. It includes the name of the office bearers, the number of bodies and units and date of the formal establishment of the party. As a response to the application for registration Election Commission asked the President of the party to appear himself physically or authorized persons before the Commission on 22nd December 1993 at 3 p.m.[7] Accordingly the party was represented by Prof. Gangmumei Kamei President, Shri M. Maringa Vice President and . Shri S.H. Seipu General Secretary.[8] Again on 21st December 1993 Shri S.H. Seipu the General Secretary of the party again submitted another application with some more information about the number of primary and active members and number of 'District' and 'Kendra Committees.'[9] He also requested the Commission to examine all the necessary information for a favourable action. Thus after the fulfilment of all required formalities the Election Commission officially permitted to give a provisional registration under section 29 A of the Representation of People Act, 1951, as a political party.

This was effected from the 22nd December 1993.[10] However, in regard to the reservation of symbol the Commission stated that "the registration will not entitle to the party to the reservation of any exclusive symbol for it. However, the candidates duly set-up by the party at an election will be entitled to benefits of paragraph 12 of the Election Symbol (Reservation and Allotment) Order 1968." Thus within a short days of its establishment the party was able to get provisional registration from the Election Commission of the Government of India.

FIRST CONVENTION OF THE PARTY 1994

The first political convention of Federal Party of Manipur was held on 21st October 1994. For the party it was a very important political development that it made a turning point in the history of the party. In the Special General Body meeting which was held in the previous year had laid a basic theoretical and ideological foundation for the existence as a political party. But this convention again brought a new dimension in the political activities of the party by consolidating and strengthening her ideology.

The meeting was held at Gandhi Memorial Hall. It was a well-attended meeting. About 1150 delegates from all the districts were assembled and participated in the deliberation. The convention was inaugurated by Prof. Gangmumei Kamei, the president of the party with a flag hoisting ceremony. The following resolutions were adopted.

Agenda No. 1:

The whole body of the resolutions was divided into three agendas. The first agenda was on political issues. The basic objective of the party as stated above is to restructure the Indian polity on the federal principle and autonomy for the state of Manipur. Therefore in the resolution the party again put a demand to restructure the Indian polity on Federal structure. In the process of discussion every delegates had expressed their concerned at the dilution of the federal principle. They were of the view that this situation was created due to the control of Central Government by a highly 'Centralised and monolithic'[12] political party like the Indian National Congress. The members who participated in the deliberation also had pointed out that the policy of centralism of the Congress Party i.e., the ruling party had encroached upon the principle of 'Federalism' underlying the Indian polity and ultimately it led to the weakening of the state.

At the same time the delegates also bitterly criticized the Indian National Congress for their hegemonic and undemocratic ethos. They were of the view that this party represents the capitalist and chauvinistic interest and always protected the interest of Indian Constitution specially Article 356 which was taken by the convention as a serious instrument for the interference and encroachment in the autonomy of the states of the Indian Federation. The distortion and destruction of federal principle by creating a 'LEVIATHAN' known as Center was regarded by the members as an undemocratic policy.

On the other hand the members also expressed their happiness and satisfaction at the emergence of the idea of regionalism among the minds of the people. They felt that it would be a dialectical response to the 'hegemonic interventionist and interfering action of all Central Government.'[13] It was a convincing opinion of all the members that regionalism was the healthy and constructive force in the body politic of the country. It was also believed that regionalism would strengthen the Indian unity and its multi-nationality nationhood. In this connection the meeting also put some observation about the role to be played by various ethnic, political and revolutionary movements in the process of the nation building. Therefore they expressed their positive view that they should be accommodated within the federal framework by giving autonomy and self-government to the people of the states and regions.

By recalling the whole history of the evolution of state of Manipur from small kingdom of Kangla to full fledged sovereign state in 15th century, an empire in the 18th century maintaining her sovereignty till the British conquest of 1891, and regaining her political autonomy under the Manipur State Constitution Act 1947 with a constitutional monarchy, followed by a long spell of Indian Government's rule and giving a statehood in 1972, the delegates put a strong observation in the unhealthy relationship between center and Manipur State. Therefore they expressed their desire to secure for Manipur a rightful and dignified place in the Indian Republic on the principle of federalism. They were of the view that the principle of restructure of relationship between Manipur and Centre would be based on federal principle and more autonomy for the state with full recognition of the 'historical prerogative of Manipur'.[14]

On the basis of these observations and arguments the convention also criticized the hegemonic and centralist forces threatening the democratic and federal base of Indian Polity. In addition to this the delegates, after having a detail discussion about the relationship between Centre and Manipur, had expressed their concern to the immediate need to review the present political trend. Accordingly this convention on the basis of the above mentioned nature of deliberation had adopted the following political resolutions. They were: -

(A) Equal Representation of the States in the Parliament

Federal Party of Manipur is of the view that since India is a union of States as mentioned in Article I of the Indian Constitution, there should be an equal representation of the states in the parliament, irrespective of their size and population. The party felt that if there is an equality in the number of a representation in the parliament there would be an equal voice among the states. The present system of representation which is on the basis of population was treated by the party as a serious violation to the principle of federalism. It was also suggested that this chamber of the house should be made all-powerful. However, Federal Party of Manipur was not against the having of another chamber of legislative body constituted by the members which were elected on the basis of population. The adoption of this resolution was a major step of the party towards the demand for the restructuring of Centre and State relationship.

(B) More power for the State

The ideological foundation of the Federal Party of Manipur was to change the nature of relationship between Centre and State. Therefore they demanded to restructure the system centre and state relationship. This aspect was again raised in this convention. In the process of the adoption of this resolution the members pointed out the nature of the distribution of powers between the centre and state as set out in Part XI of the Indian Constitution specially Article 246 and Seventh Schedule. However, the party expressed their reservation to the control of the union over the states as provided in Article 356. Therefore the party demanded that this provision should be removed and the nature of the distribution of powers between Centre and State as mentioned in Seventh Schedule should be restructured.

In this regard the convention of the party proposed that the Union List with 96 subjects should be reduced and the subjects like, defence, foreign affairs, communications, Finance and Currency Central Legislative Affairs, Central Judiciary affairs and Union Public Service should be confined in List No. I of the Centre. It is also proposed that all the subjects given in the List No. II and those not covered in the Union List should be transferred to the states and 'List No. III' i.e. Concurrent 'List' should be abolished and all the subjects of this List should be transferred to the States list.

The demand for the abolition of Article 356 of the Indian Constitution was also another notable political step of Federal Party of Manipur. The party appreciates the spirit of the provision of emergency power conferred on the Union Government under Part XVIII of the constitution. But the party felt that this provision was misused by the Union Government on narrow political considerations by the ruling parties in the Centre. The party thinks that this system is repugnant to the federal democratic ethos of the Indian polity. On the basis of this argument the convention strongly demanded to abolish Article 356 to ensure freedom, democracy and federalism in the Indian Union.

Federal Party of Manipur was also very much particular in the style of functioning of Finance Commission and Planning Commission. The party was of the opinion that the Finance Commission is a statutory body provided by the constitution of India whereas the Planning Commission is a body constituted by an executive decision of the Government of India. From the constitutional point of view Finance Commission should have more financial power than planning commission. But the planning commission has enjoyed the power of fund granting facilities. This body was managed and controlled by the Union Government. The party was of the view that under this policy the Central Government has established its own primacy and hegemony over the state by playing havoc with development plans and autonomy of the state. As a result of this the position of Finance Commission had been belittled by the Central Government. Keeping this view into consideration the convention unanimously resolved to propose that "the Finance Commission has to be strengthened and National Development Council and the Planning Commission should be made constitutional and statutory bodies with powers to decide and distribute funds and ensure planning on national basis to the states."[15]

(C) Autonomy of the State of Manipur

The style of the provision of autonomy as given in the Indian constitution was thoroughly discussed in the convention. The members were of the view that the present pattern of autonomy for the state was not uniform. The meeting had pointed out two cases i.e. the special status for Jammu and Kashmir State under Article 370 and special autonomy for Nagaland state under Art.371-A. In this connection all the members of the convention were of the opinion that keeping in view of the extraordinary circumstances of the merger of Manipur into India the patterns of autonomy for Manipur should be a combination of the spirit of Art.370 and Art.371.

In the context of this observation the convention was of the opinion that "the Manipur State Constitution Act 1947 which was in operation in Manipur prior to the merger into the Indian Dominion on 15, October 1949 (and which has not been revoked formally) should be the basis of the autonomy of Manipur".[16] The members also expressed the immediate need to renegotiate between Manipur and Central Government on this vital constitutional issue. Majority of the members proposed that the special autonomy under Art. 371(A) given to Nagaland should be made applicable to Manipur also.

In addition to this the party also resolved to demand for the introduction of autonomy in different levels of administrative units like District level, Zilla Parishad level and Gram Panchayat level. Here the party demanded that Six Schedule of the Indian Constitution should be introduced in the hill districts of Manipur, the provisions of the 73rd amendment of the constitution should be made functional with necessary amendments and the village Authority Act, 1956 operating in the hill areas should be reviewed or replaced by a suitable law in commensurate with the spirit and letters of the Manipur Hill people's Regulation, 1947.

Apart from the issue of the restructuring of centre and state relationship and autonomy of the state of Manipur this convention also expressed their concern on the issue of the possibilities for the co-existence and harmonious relationship among the different ethnic groups in the state. So in order to ensure harmonious relationship and a sense of belonging among the people of Manipur the convention resolved to demand for the establishment of an 'Inter-Ethnic Council' in Manipur.

Then to protect the basic human rights of the people of Manipur the convention resolved to demand for the establishment of a state level 'Human Rights Commission' on the pattern of National Human Rights Commission.

Indeed, the idea for the establishments of "Inter Ethnic Council" and State Human Rights Commission was a remarkable political decision of Federal Party of Manipur Before this no other political parties raised this issue for a positive social development in the state.

Agenda 2: Economic Resolutions.

The Federal Party of Manipur firmly believed that the political development or positive political changes would not be possible without strong economic foundation. And to maintain equilibrium in the plural society would be possible only when there is a social justice and equitable development. On the basic foundation of this understanding Federal Party of Manipur was firmly committed to build up an egalitarian society based on development with social justice and on equitable development in different regions.

In the context of Manipur, Federal Party of Manipur was of the view that despite the completion of several Five Years Plans the Manipur state was not able to reach to a stage, which could sustain itself. Due to this condition there was big developmental gap between Manipur and other states in widening over the years. On the other hand the unsystematic and bad planning since 1951 the state was not able to lay any foundation for long-term development. The failure on the part of plan efforts so far, had stopped the scope for additional resource mobilization in the state was shrinking. Therefore, the Federal party of Manipur, in order to have a capability to regenerate the economic position of Manipur, made a quite logical and reasonable proposal to make one time huge financial investment. The party had categorically pointed out that such type of big push in the financial investment was necessary to the development of the State.

Besides this the convention also discussed the economic benefits given by the New Economic Policy to the state. It was also pointed out that this policy had two components.One component aims towards the stabilization of price and exchange rates and other aims, to endeavours to bring about structural transformation of the economy. The Federal Party of Manipur felt that during the interim period of structural adjustment the poor state tend to suffer. Therefore the party resolved to make a proposal to implement the principle of special programme for the state of Manipur during the adjustment period.

The party also thought that the opening of trade relationship between India and Myanmar through Manipur would be a great advantageous position for the improvement of financial condition of this state. Therefore the party proposed that the State Government should adopt specific short-term policies to reap the benefits of the border trade.

Agenda 3: Resolution on Social Federalism

It is a known fact that without stability and peace in the society no nation and no state could march forward to the progress of political development. Therefore in order to have a positive progress in the political life of the state there should be a social cohesiveness and spirit of co-existence among the people. However, to bring this idea is not an easy task particularly to the state where the pluralistic society exists.

The Federal Party of Manipur was also fully aware of the fact that Manipur society is a plural society where the different ethnic groups, cultures and languages flourished right from the early historical period. It is also true that this ethnic cultural and linguistic pluralism have played and will continue to play an important role in social development. However, the party had fully realized that there were a lot of variations and social injustices in the process of the co-existence among the ethnic group of people. The feeling of the losing of their distinctive identity in the hand of big group is one of the greatest apprehensive factors among the small group of people. In this respect, the unanimous view of the party was that every ethnic group should have the privilege to preserve their identity within the framework of Manipuri society. And the bigger group should have the respect to the historical identity of the interest of small group.

Keeping these observations into consideration the Federal Party of Manipur was of the view that "social federalism can best ensure and safeguard the multiple interests of different ethnic groups."[17] And in order to materialize the concept of 'social federalism' the convention had proposed some measures like "consistent application of the principle of actual quality, the granting of adequate autonomy, equal rights for all the ethnic groups big or small, suppression of any form of exploitation and discrimination, a truly democratic and federalistic state structure that generates the equal development of ethnic minorities, absence of compulsion in dealing with language question, respect for the other culture, customary and traditional practices, complete trust and mutual co-operation among all the peoples so as to prevent the internal and external reactionary forces from taking advantage of the pluralistic nature of the society."[18]

Then after having a detail discussion the members unanimously agreed to resolve for a united and resolute struggle to achieve the following conditions for the establishment of the idea of 'social federalism'.

The conditions were:

(a) Equality at the individual and collective levels;

(b) Cultural identity of all the ethnic groups;

(c) Social Harmonisation;

(d) Equitable Economic development;

(e) Protection of ethnic minorities; and

(f) Protection of basic human rights.

Indeed, the first convention was very significant political step for Federal Party of Manipur. That it pledged to secure a rightful and dignified place within the framework of Indian Constitution. The demand to recognize the 'historical prerogative of Manipur' was undoubtedly a great challenge to the attitude of the deliberate ignorance of the centralist elements of the Government of India. Apart from the political issue this convention also proposed to introduce an equitable economic distribution system on the basic of the need of the state whatever the size may be. The economic resolution adopted by the convention to provide one time a big financial investment for the regeneration of the economic position of Manipur and for having the capability of herself generating economic conditions indeed was a unique political step of Federal Party of Manipur. After having this idea, now it became a serious debatable issue among the social scientist and economists of the state. On the other hand it is also a big ideological contribution of the party to the future generation people of the state. The concept of 'Social Federalism' was also a new idea proposed by FPM. This social idea could be implemented in the larger context of Indian society. Therefore the first convention of 1994 was a very important political step of FPM because after this the party was able to penetrate even into the inner circle of the society with its basic ideological principles and objectives. Thus from this day the party began to plant the ideological trees of the ideas of 'Federalism and Autonomy' 'Self Generating Economic life' and 'Social Federalism' in the fervent political soil of Manipur.

GENERAL ELECTION OF 1995

For Federal Party of Manipur the election of 1995 was a very important political step. The participation in this election was, in fact, a preparatory step for a long political journey of this party. It was also viewed that the participation of the party in this election was also another preparatory step for a new and social order in Manipur.[19] On the other hand this election also was a great boon in disguise for the party because it laid a strong foundation for the recognition of this party as an important regional political force of the state. The ideological objective of the party was clearly mentioned right from the very inception. So the party participated in the election under the ideological banner of 'federalism and autonomy'. Besides this the party also put some important issues for the state of Manipur which were widely welcomed by the people and it became a serious debatable issue among the common people.

'FEDERALISM IS THE NEED OF THE HOUR, AND AUTONOMY FOR OUR IDENTITY' was the main slogan of Federal Party of Manipur in this election. Under this plank the party presented a manifesto on two important aspects. The first part of the manifesto dealt with the general ideological objectives in which the party strongly emphasized for the 'restructuring of the Indian polity' on the line of federalism and autonomy of the states. The second part was on some important issues of Manipur which was considered as the vital points for her future history. The whole resolutions which were passed by the 1st convention of 1994 was fully incorporated in the first part of the manifesto. The party placed give two issues as the focal points for the better life of future Manipur and also makes some other points, which were directly related with the developmental aspect of the state.

'Territorial integrity and unity of Manipur was a very important issue for every social, political and voluntary organisation of the state of Manipur. Federal Party of Manipur was also fully awared of the fact that this issue was developed just after the completion of the merger of Manipur into India. A serious threat to the territorial integrity of Manipur and unity of the people was a very apprehensive point in every mind of the people of Manipur. It is also a fact that every political, social and voluntary organisation was against any type of disturbances in the territorial integrity and unity of the people of Manipur. But the party felt that to make a continuous shouting against the possible danger of the threat of territorial integrity of the state was not a practical political step. It was an accepted view of all the members of the party that territorial boundary of any state would be properly guarded and protected only by the people not any other else. It was also believed that the people who have the sense of belongingness would be able to protect the territory and to preserve the unity. In this respect the party, in its manifesto presented a new and the highly thought provoking slogan i.e. 'LIVE FRONTIER POLICY'[20] to the people of Manipur for continuous debate among them. The justification of the party in the new idea was that if there were no proper administrative functioning, no proper attention to the people of border areas, no welfare policy adopted for the better life of the people, the possibility for the growth of the sense of belongingness among the people of border areas would not able to come up to a certain expectation level. Therefore the party in her manifesto strongly emphasized that they would initiate a 'Live Frontier Policy' by opening many avenues for the welfare of the people of border area. It was also mentioned that this policy would be able to protect the boundaries of Manipur.

Negotiation for solution of revolutionary movements was another important issue of focal points highlighted by the FPM in its manifesto. It is a universal law and historical truth that all form of conflict are resolved on the negotiation tables .It was the strong view of the party that since the objective of the revolutionary movements was for the establishment of a separate distinctive political identity outside the constitution of India, it was not practicable to initiate for a dialogue within the framework of the Indian Constitution. This was also the opinion of the party that the talk with revolutionary movements should be initiated without any condition. Therefore in its manifesto the party proposed that there should be a negotiation between the Government of India and various revolutionary groups. It was also emphasized that in the process of peace the services of persons of good will and recognized credibility of national and international status will be sought and made available to the negotiating position.

In addition to this the party also strongly asserted its firm stands for the protection of basic human rights of the people. In this regard the party demanded the following issues i.e. the establishment of Human Rights Commission for the state of Manipur, withdrawal of draconian laws like 'Armed Forces Special Power Act, TADA and Punjab Security Act. The party also felt that the revolutionary movement aims for a political cause. Therefore the political prisoners status should be given for the insurgents of various groups arrested or imprisoned by the state.

Besides this the issues like the social unity and the cultural identity of the people of Manipur, the establishment of Inter-Ethnic Council to deal with ethnic and communal problems of the state, development with social justice etc. were also categorically pointed out with logical argument in the manifesto. One of the most important outstanding issues, which were clearly mentioned in the manifesto in connection with the developmental aspect of the state, was the idea for the expansion of National History No.53. FPM promised "National History 53 will be expanded to be the greater lifeline of Manipur as NH 39 is no longer dependable supply line for Manipur". [21]

Thus, with these specific issue and agendas the Federal Party of Manipur participated in this 6th General Election of Manipur Legislative Assembly. This was the maiden election battle of the party. Therefore the party was not interested to contest from every assembly segments. However due to the absence of formal recognition from the Election Commission the candidates of Federal Party of Manipur was not able to contest under the same symbol. So, in order to get the opportunity to participate under a common symbol the party submitted a panel of symbol from among the reserve symbol of the Election Commission such as (i) Elephant (ii) Lion (iii) Rising sun behind the hills to the office of Chief Electorate Officer, Government of Manipur. The party had concentrated only in some assembly segments. Indeed, this election was a grand success of the party. In her maiden election battle the Federal Party of Manipur was able to open its political account by securing two seats and in most of the assembly constituencies the party candidates were defeated by a narrow margin. In fact, analyzing from the performance of the election it can be suggested that this election was a remarkable achievement of the party. In its victory meeting the president of the party expressed their gratitude to the people of Manipur for extending their full co-operation and for giving recognition to the party.At the same time the party also expressed their full satisfaction to the people for their warm receipt to the ideology and. They also asserted that 'Federal Party of Manipur is no doubt, a local party with national outlook. So, this election paved a very big way for having a long and bright future political journey in the body polity of the Federation of Indian Democracy.

FORMAL RECOGNISATION AND ALLOTMENT OF SYMBOL

After getting the result of the 6th General Election of Manipur and degree of their poll performance the party had submitted a formal request to recognize the Federal Party of Manipur as the political party under the provision of law. The action of the Election commission was so prompt that in an official notification dated 30th October 1995 the Commission formally recognized Federal Party of Manipur as a state based political party.

In their official notification the Commission said that while reviewing the poll performance of the political parties at the general election to the legislative assembly of Manipur held in Feb- March 1995 in the terms of paras 6 and 7 of the Election Symbols (Reservation and Allotment order 1968), the Election Commission was satisfied to the poll performance of Federal Party of Manipur. Therefore under the terms of Para 6(2) of the election symbol (Reservation and Allotment} order 1968 the FPM was eligible for recognisation as a state political party with this observation the election commission allotted the symbol of 'Rising Sun' to FPM in the state of Manipur. The official notification of the allotment of recognized symbol was communicated on 31st Oct. 1995 to the General Secretary of party.

Thus, with this official notification Federal Party of Manipur became a state based political party.

REFERENCES

1. Presidential Address on Special Session of the General Assembly of Federal Party of Manipur, Imphal, 9th November 1993.
2. Ibid.
3. Ibid.
4. Ibid.
5. Proceedings of the Special Session of the General Assembly of Federal Party of Manipur held on 9th Nov. 1993.
6. Applications submitted to Election Commission for registration as a political Party end—section 29 (A) of the Representation of the people Act 1951.
7. Ref. No. 56/164/93 J.S. II/3019 dated 23rd November 1993 Letter from Sobon Lal Chand, Under Secy. (Legal) to Prof. Gangmumei President FPM.
8. Ref. FPM /RE/1-93-94 dated 10.12.1993 Letter to Under Secy. (Legal) from President FPM.
9. Ref. No. FPM/RE/i/93-94 Dated 12-12-93 Letter from General Secy. FPM to Secy. Election Commission

10. Ref. No. 56 /164/93/J.S.II dated 23rd December 1993 letter from under secy.(Legal) of Election Commission Govt. Of India to Prof. Gangmumei Kamei.
11. Ibid
12. Federalism and Autonomy for Manipur (Resolution of the First Convention of FPM.) p. 1
13. Ibid. p. 2
14. Ibid. p. 3
15. Ibid. p.6
16. Ibid.
17. Ibid. p. 10
18. Ibid.
19. The Federal Manifesto 1995. p. 5
20. Ibid.
21. Ibid. p. 10
22. Letter from Gangmumei President FPM to the Chief Election Office Govt. of Manipur vide no. FPM/Symbol/95 dated 17.1.1995.
23. See Appendix No. 3
24. No 56/95/J.S II/ 1866 dated 31st October 1995 letter from BN Chaula Uner Secy. to the General Secy. Federal Party of Manipur.

CHAPTER FOUR

PARTICIPATION IN THE GOVERNANCE

A. PARTICIPATION IN MINISTRY FORMATION.

The positive impact and significance of the 'Sixth General Election' of the Manipur Legislative Assembly, particularly in relation with the political development of Federal Party of Manipur, has already been discussed in the previous chapter. To get a formal recognition as a political party under the legal provision of the Election Commission of India was the most important positive impact produced by the result of election to Federal Party of Manipur. In this Sixth General Election the Federal Party of Manipur had contested in 22(twenty-two) assembly constituencies and in her maiden election battle she was able to get two seats. Prof. Gangmumei Kamei, President of the party was elected from the Nungba Assembly Constituency (ST) and Dr. W. Thoiba Singh from Heingang Assembly Constituency. In most of the assembly segments where the party had contested, her official candidates were able to give a very good performance though they were defeated by narrow margins.

The people's verdict in the Sixth General Election was in favour of a coalition ministry in the state. Therefore, the post-election scenario was a very important issue for every political party in the state. The Federal Party of Manipur also took it as a very important political step.

Since no political party was in a position to form a ministry every political parties in the state was prepared for a coalition ministry. This political development was a great concern to Federal Party of Manipur also. Accordingly a series of serious discussions was going on in the party on the issue of what would be the stand of the party in this present political scenario. After having a long discussion a consensus opinion was arrived at among the members that it would be the duty of the party to pay respect and honour the verdict of the people. The members were of the view that since the verdict of the people was for a coalition government the party should actively participate and involve in the process of the governance of the state. In the meantime invitations were also received from other political parties to join in the process of the formation of ministry in their favour. One group was led by Congress Party and another by Manipur People's Party. At last the party had decided to support the Congress led coalition group under some concrete understanding. In a statement the Federal Party of Manipur had categorically mentioned the basic reasons of their joining in the formation of coalition ministry. They said,

> "without prejudice to the socio-economic and political ideology contained in the manifesto of the Federal Party of Manipur the party stands for restructuring of Indian polity on the basis of federalism in general and for full autonomy of Manipur and preservation of her territorial integrity and the unity of her people with a concept of 'LIVE FRONTIER POLICY' in particular. With this basic understanding the FPM supports the Congress led ministry in order to fulfill the mandate of the people in the following conditions, failing which, the FPM shall have the right to withdraw from the ministry at any moment."[1]

On the basis of this conceptual principle the party placed 10(ten) points, which were to be fulfilled by the new ministry. The points were:

(a) Expansion of the National Highway No. 53.

(b) Rectification of the negative effects of the Loktak Hydro Electric Project.

(c) Shifting of the Assam Rifles or any other security forces from Kangla.

(d) Establishment of Human Rights Commission for the State of Manipur and withdrawal of draconian laws like Armed Forces Special Power Act, TADA, Punjab Security Act.

(e) Immediate implementation of Government recommendation on O.B.C.

(f) Establishment of an Inter-Ethnic Council.

(g) Pension for members of District Council, Zilla Parishad, Municipality, Pramukh and Pradhan

(h) Non-alienation and transfer of lands from the indigenous people to the non-indigenous migrants, framing of land laws suitable to tribal and hill areas and all khast land should be made available for agricultural purposes.

(i) A massive employment generating schemes for the educated unemployed youths and for the weaker sections of the society.

(j) Negotiation between the Government of India and various revolutionary groups by involving the services of persons of goodwill and recognized credibility of national and international stature.

Accordingly the president of the party had formally communicated these conditions to the leader of the Congress Legislature Party. Thus under a formal understanding the two elected members of the party had joined the ministry headed by the Congress Party. Both the elected members of the party was given the ministerial position in the ministry. One was in the rank of cabinet minister with the portfolio of Higher Education and Science and Technology and other in the rank of state minister to look after the Tourism affairs. Thus with this participation the FPM had started her political journey by involving in the governance of the state.

Then within a very short time a serious internal political crisis had developed among the coalition partners of the ministry. As a result of this other political parties in the ministry including Federal Party of Manipur had formed a new political front entitled "United Democratic Front" and immediately they withdrew their support from the Congress led ministry under the leadership of Shri Rishang Keishing. The 'Front' was constituted by 1. Progressive Janata Dal, 2. NPP, 3. Samata Party, 4. Federal Party of Manipur, 5. Janata Dal, 6. Independent MLA. In their memorandum which was submitted to the Governor of Manipur, they alleged that " the credibility of Shri Rishang Keishing as Chief Minister has not been accepted by the people of Manipur due to his narrow and partisan outlook influence by his coterie of so called 'Party Leaders"[2]. Apart from this they also claimed that Shri Rishang Keishing was not able to enforce a strong will of administration on the issue of Kuki-Naga conflict. The failure in the enforcement of the administrative will and open defiance by the people of these two communities were mainly because of the lack of credibility of the leader of the Congress led government. They had also pointed out that Shri Rishang Keishing had "elusively sidelined the issue of the shifting of security forces from the Kangla Fort and establishment of State Human Rights Commission for which he gave assurances in the floor of the Manipur Assembly"[3] .In addition to this the memorandum also stressed the failure of the leader of the ministry to maintain law and order in the state. With these allegations and assessments they informed the Governor of the State about the withdrawal of their support to the Congress led ministry. Further they had also requested His Excellency the Governor of Manipur to invite United Legislative Front (ULF) to form a new ministry. Shri R.K Ranbir Singh was the leader of ULF.

The memorandum was signed by 9 (nine) M.L.A.s including the two members of Federal Party of Manipur. They also sent another copy of memorandum to the Speaker of the Manipur Legislative Assembly for his information. However, all kinds of political manouvering initiated by the 'Front' to remove the Congress led government were not clicked in a positive direction. And they were compelled by the existing political circumstances to wait for an opportune time. Thus, just after the withdrawal of the support to the Congress led ministry, the FPM began to play the role of the opposition from July 1995 to December 1997. During this period the party had played a major constructive role as a responsible opposition party by participating in every issue of the state and by focusing the issues of her political agendas in the floor of the Legislative Assembly[4].

(B) PARLIAMENTARY ELECTION, 1996

The parliamentary election of 1996 was a great landmark of Federal Party of Manipur in the journey of her political activities. This election was, indeed, a boon in disguise of the party that it greatly rendered a significant contribution in the strengthening of the party's position in the political arena of the state. No doubt this election gave an ample opportunely to the party to expand her organizational activities throughout the entire areas of the state. At the same time the party also was able to expand her ideological principles and objectives in every nook and corner of the state. The party leaders felt that the parliamentary election was a great challenge to the Federal Party of Manipur that the result of the performance of the party would make a deciding factor for having a successful future political life of the party. Therefore the party leaders, keeping all these aspects in their mind, had decided to contest both the parliamentary seats of Manipur. Shri Nongmaithem Chittaranjan Singh popularly known as N. Pahari Singh, a noted singer and a social worker of his time was selected as the candidate of the party to contest the election from the Inner Manipur

Parliamentary Constituency and Shri Shimerio Shaiza popularly known as Major Shaiza, a retired army officer and younger brother of late Shri Yangmaso Shaiza the former Chief Minister of Manipur, from Outer Parliamentary Constituency.

Like the general election of 1995 this time also the Federal Party Manipur had entered into the election battlefield under the banner of her ideological principles of federalism and autonomy. The party again had strongly reiterated the immediate need for the emergence of the concept regionalism in the Indian politics. The strong view of the party was that, "in the context of the ongoing nation building process in the country, the emergence of regionalism is a dialectical response to the hegemonic centralism of the Government of India controlled by the capitalistic and chauvinistic vested interest of Indian upper caste and classes."[5] The party also claimed that her only desire was to shape a new future political destiny of Manipur and secured for her people. "a rightful and dignified place in the Indian Republic. Thus with some basic ideological frameworks like Federalism, Autonomy and Self-Government with Social Justice, Social Federalism, the party put some more agendas for having debates on every aspects of the state among the people of Manipur.

The issues like the questions of the restructuring of the Indian polity on the principles of federalism, the equal representation of the states to Federal Parliament, the restructuring of the Constitution of India on the issue of the division of power between the Federal Government and States, the abrogation of Article 356 which was treated by the party as an instrument of Central Government's intervention in the states to suit the interest of the ruling party in the Center, were the main basic features highlighted in the manifesto of the Federal Party of Manipur . In regard to the autonomy for Manipur the party again had reiterated that there should be a renegotiation between India and Manipur on the basis of the pre merger political status of Manipur as provided in the Manipur State Constitution Act 1947 and the Stand Still Agreement, 1947 and Instrument of Accession, 1947. The other agendas which were mentioned in the manifesto were District and Village level autonomy, Clear-cut legal position of Finance Commission and Planning Commission, Integrity and unity of Manipur, social harmony and peaceful resolution for solution of revolutionary movements without precondition. Apart from this the party also mentioned some basic developmental agendas like improvement of transport and communication system, tourism industry, proper management of environmental and ecology system, rehabilitation of people affected by Loktak Project. One of the most important notable features of the manifesto of the party was its demand for a third Lok Sabha seat for Manipur. The Federal Party of Manipur was of the view that the present nature of the formation of parliamentary constituency segment could not be applicable in the context of Manipur. Therefore the party proposed for another parliamentary seat in the future delimitation of the area of parliamentary constituency. In fact this demand was in tune with the desire of the people of Manipur. Along with this the party also proposed to create a Legislative Council for Manipur. It was a noteworthy political proposal of the party which no other political parties had reflected so far in their election manifesto. The party felt that under the present system of election there was no room for getting opportunity to represent the constituency by the minority section and small communities section of the people. On the basis of this idea the party proposed for the creation of a 45(forty five) members Legislative Council in Manipur with one-third representation for women and un represented communities of the state.[6]

Thus under the banner of a clear cut ideological principles and political issues the Federal Party Manipur had launched a large-scale election campaign in both parliamentary constituencies. Compared with the nature of the election campaign of other political parties, the Federal Party Manipur had an opportunity to march ahead so far the degree of election tempo was concerned. Two factors were responsible for this positive development. One was the ideology, objective and issues placed by the party for public debate and another was the personnel popularity of the candidates. The ideological principles and objectives, as has already been mentioned in the previous chapters, was a new political concept at least to the common people. Of course it was not a new idea to the educated people but to make these theoretical concepts, as an objective of a political party and the demand for the restructuring of the whole body of Indian polity was a new political dimension, which had never experienced in the past by the people of Manipur. Therefore when these issues were placed for discussion in public platform, it becomes an interesting topic for debate among the people and it was also warmly well received by many section of the society. The fundamental issues of the state of that time like the question of 'the territorial integrity and unity of the people, the protection of basic human right, formation of Inter Ethnic Council etc. were the main points focused by the party to the knowledge of the people. The idea of the principle of 'Live Frontier Policy' of the party had given an opportunity to the people who involved in the making of policy decision of the state to review their concept of 'territorial integrity and unity of the people.' Thus these ideological principles and basic issues had rendered an opportunity to the party to expand her political activities in every areas of the state. At the same time the party was also able to emerge as a responsible political organisation in the political platform of the state. These ideological principles and issue based on agendas was the solid contribution of the party to their candidates in the process of parliamentary election.

Particularly in the context of Manipur the ideological principles and objectives could not be the only factor in the winning process of the election. People always keep their value to the personal popularity of the candidates. As has already been mentioned above about Shri N. Chittaranjan Singh (N.Pahari) as a noted singer and a social activist. His name was not a new to every people of Manipur. At the same time during his youthful days he was actively involved in many social activities which was directly or indirectly related with the political movement launched for the preservation of national identity of Manipuri people. From these backgrounds the people had a very good impression about the sincerity, integrity and capabilities of Shri N. Chittaranjan Singh (Pahari Singh). In every election meeting he was able to attract the attention of the crowd. He was able to get support even from many quarters by crossing the party line. Thus the Federal Party Manipur was able to give a very good fight in the election of the Inner Manipur Parliamentary constituency.

Shri Shimrio Shaiza popularly known as Major Shaiza was also a popular personality. He was a man of principle and a spokesman for territorial integrity and unity of the people of Manipur. He was an open minded man. He had a peculiar character of frankness when he dealt with the common people. Indeed, the selection of Shri Shaiza as the official candidate of Federal Party of Manipur was good opportunity for the party to extend her political activities and ideological principles in other hill areas of the state. The issues like the suitable land laws for the hill areas, protection of human rights etc. had created a very good impression about the party in the minds of the hill people. Thus under the banner of federalism and autonomy the party was able to give a very good fight in these parliamentary constituency also.

The official result of the election was not in favour of the Federal Party of Manipur. All the candidates of the party were defeated with a narrow margin. But it was a great moral and ideological victory of the party. After this election the confidence of the people towards the party was tremendously increased. They began to create an impression that the Federal Party of Manipur was the only political forum which stands for regional issues of North East India in general and Manipur in particular. In this parliamentary election the party got 13.5% of the of the total vote polled. Thus, the parliamentary election of 1996 was a great landmark of the Federal Party of Manipur.

(C) FORMATION OF UNITED FRONT MINISTRY 1997.

In the year 1997 the 'Front Ministry' led by Rishang Keishing was collapsed and split into two. It also effects the congress organization. A sizeable section of the members of the Congress Party came out under the leadership of Shri. W. Nipamacha Singh, the Speaker of the Legislative Assembly and formed a new local party known as 'Manipur State Congress Party' (MSCP). Then in order to form a new ministry a political front was formed consisting of MSCP, MPP, CPI and FPM. It was known as 'United Front' and Shri W. Nipamacha Singh was elected as the leader of it. Immediately after the formation of this coalition front he claimed to form a new ministry. Thus the 'United Front Ministry' was formed with Shri W. Nipamacha Singh as Chief Minister. In this ministry Federal Party of Manipur was also participated. The Federal Party of Manipur claimed that the toppling of 'Congress Ministry'[7] was a great victory over the 'centralist and hegemonic' forces represented by the Congress I government.

In a press release issued on 24-12-1997 Federal Party of Manipur claimed that the disintegration of the Congress was a triumph of regionalism in Manipur politics."[8] It was also mentioned that Federal Party of Manipur was fighting against the colonial tendencies from mainland India. Therefore as a mark of protest against the hegemonistic political culture of Congress Party, it withdrew from the ministry .It is also said that FPM was actively involved in the toppling of the Congress I ministry and formation of new ministry. To see the active involvement of the Federal Party in the toppling of Congress ministry, Shri W. Nipamacha Singh had invited the party MLAs to join the new ministry. The Federal Party of Manipur was very much concerned about the stability of the new ministry. Therefore they were of the view that a new ministry would not be possible unless all the regional political forces were united. So they also suggested to invite Manipur People's Party in the new ministry.[9] FPM was of the view that the collapse of Congress ministry was a victory of regional force. So MPP and other regional political parties should take advantage of the emerging political scenario. Further the party also expressed their concern at the norms of a coalition of ministry particularly. The party expressed its reservation at the avoiding nature of Manipur State Congress at the decision of the core committee. The party was of the view that "such a stance intentionally or inadvertently will encourage the CLP under a new and ambitious leader to induce wedge into the intra-coalition partnership relationship."[10] With this critical observation the party also kept its commitment to the United Front Ministry and expressed their desire to thrash out the issues within the 'Front'. Thus on the basis of this understanding and commitment Federal Party of Manipur, in its Working Committee meeting held on 9th December, 1997 at 7.30 A.M, resolved to direct the Federal Legislative Wing to participate in the ministry led by W. Nipamacha keeping in view the assurances given by the leader of the Manipur State Congress to the party.[11]

D. THE BYE ELECTION OF 1998.

The bye-election of Tadubi Assembly Constituency was another significant feature of the political development of Federal Party of Manipur. In the general election of 1995 this assembly constituency was represented by one Mr. O. Lohri. But his membership was disqualified by the Speaker of the Assembly on the basis of some legal standpoints. As a result of this disqualification of membership the seat of Tadubi assembly constituency was lying vacant. Accordingly the Election Commission of India had issued a notification for conducting the bye-election. At that time an underground-outfit of the Naga inhabited areas had strongly opposed any type of democratic practices of the Indian Government. Therefore they asked all the Naga people not to contest any type of election, which was held under the Constitution of India. They also warned that they would give a severe punishment to those Naga people who filed nomination paper for election in the bye-election of Tadubi Assembly Constituency. Thus a fear psychosis was created among the Naga people. So they were not prepared to file the nomination paper to contest the election. The Manipur State Congress Party who was a major partner of United Front Ministry was also not prepared to contest the election. Even the party members from this constituency are not ready to contest the bye-election. To see this embarrassing political situation and in order to promote the value of the parliamentary democracy the party had decided to send up a candidate to contest the election from this constituency. Accordingly the Federal Party selected Shri Haokholet Kipgen, a man of Kuki tribe to contest the bye-election from this assembly constituency.

To send up a candidate of Kuki tribe to contest election from a Naga dominated assembly segment was, indeed, an extremely difficult task for the party. In the given political scenario it was a highly sensitive issue. Therefore the party leaders prepared with great care and precaution. Even to file nomination paper itself was a great problem. But anyhow the party members and volunteers were able to manage very successfully and thus he was able to submit his nomination paper in the midst of highly dangerous and difficult situation. There were two candidates. But the other candidate was rejected at the time of official scrutiny and thus he was left alone as qualified candidate. Accordingly the 'Returning Officer' declared him elected unopposed. After this victory the member of party's MLA was increased from two to three.

E. PARLIAMENTARY ELECTION OF 1999

The parliamentary election of 1999 was also another important political platform from where the Federal party of Manipur was able to demonstrate its political activities. This election was regarded by the Party as an imposition on the people of India by the impact of the failure of the national parties and their regional allies in the governance of the country. However the party thought that it was also a very good political opportunity for the Federal Party of Manipur to focus her ideas, objectives and basic principles to the common people. With these objectives she also participated in this parliamentary election by contesting in both constituencies. Captain Miss L. Sorojini Devi (Retd.) President of the 'Women Front' of the party was selected to contest from the Inner Manipur Parliamentary Constituency and Shri Gaidon Kamei, a young and an energetic social worker, who was actively involved and participated in many student organizations and youth movements and also a General Secretary of the party, was selected to contest from the Outer Manipur Parliamentary Constituency. The selection of party candidate of the party was made on the basis of two principles. In fact from the very inception the party was strongly believed that a successful working of democracy would be possible only when women were fully involved and participated in the politics. The party leader thought that this election was a good opportunity for the party to send up a women candidate so that the importance of the women would increase and more respect would be able to enjoy in the national political arenas. Secondly the party also wanted to give more emphasis on the youths, as they believed that the youths and students were the backbone of any political organisation. It was also believed that if they were moulded properly it would give an opportunity to move forward in a more positive political direction.

As usual the Federal Party of Manipur participated in the election on the basic ideological principle and objectives. Apart from the basic ideological principle of federalism and autonomy, the party also makes a solemn pledge to secure for the ancient state of Manipur, a dignified place in Federal India[13]. One of the most important basic demands was to restructure the polity of India. In addition to this the party also put some demands such as equal representation of the state to the Federal Parliament, abrogation of Art.356 etc. Besides this the party also focused on social unity and cultural identity. It was a known fact that the Federal Party of Manipur, right from the very beginning had clearly stated that one of their basic objective was to preserve and protect the social and cultural identity of various social and cultural groups. Therefore to achieve this objective in the context of the people of Manipur the party placed the following points for discussion.

They were: -

1. Development of Manipuri language which is the official language of the state included in the VIII Schedule;
2. Printing of 'Meitei Mayek' (script) in currency notes of India;
3. Financial Assistance for the establishment of Meetei Mayek Type Foundry to Manipur;
4. Development of Tribal language;
5. More programme for minorities like Manipuri speaking Muslims and tribal groups in AIR and T.V;
6. Complete eradication and prevention of HIV & AIDS;
7. Ban on the illegal entry and immigration of foreigners from Myanmars, Nepal and Bangladesh;
8. Special programmed for ST, SC and OBC of Manipur and plain tribal of Imphal valley;
9. Reservation of jobs for O.B.C;
10. Upliftment of the women, oblique and the physically handicapped and Ex-servicemen;

11. Establishment of a Women Commission for the welfare of the women;
12. Establishment of Minority Commission;[14]

Then with these issues and ideological principles the party participated in the election. In this election the party faced many practical problems during the process of election campaign particularly in Outer Parliamentary Constituency. An underground outfit boycotted this election and they even asked the Naga people not to come out and exercise their vote on the day of the election. All type of election campaigns were not allowed in the Naga inhabited areas. Therefore the party was not able to get a free movement in the election campaign .In the midst of such dangerous situation the party candidate Shri Gaidon Kamei gave a good election fight against the other political parties. No doubt the party candidates were defeated but it laid a good foundation for the party to stand as a responsible political party in the state .In regard to the relationship with other political parties the stand of the party was very clear. They said, "FPM shall strive for a stable Government with state of Manipur and will help any party which can form a stable government in the centre."[15]

(F) STATE ASSEMBLY ELECTION, 2000A.D AND PARTICIPATION IN THE MINISTRY.

The 7th 'State Assembly' was another landmark in the history of the political journey of Federal Party of Manipur. The peculiar feature of the party in this election was that this time Federal Party of Manipur did not participate in the election under her own agendas. She had participated under the banner of the 'United Front, which was constituted by two state-based political parties i.e., Manipur State Congress Party and Federal Party of Manipur. These two regional political parties were working together as hand and glove right from the time of the toppling of 'Congress Ministry' led by Shri Rishang Keishing. Therefore the two parties expressed their mutual desire to work and participate together in this election under a common agenda. In a statement on the General Election of the 7th Manipur Legislative Assembly, the President of the party had categorically stated that there would be mutual adjustment of seats between the FPM and MSCP and also there would be a friendly contest between the two parties in the ensuing general election.[16] Apart from this Federal Party of Manipur would support the MSCP party in the constituency where they did not sent up any candidate so also Manipur State Congress Party would support their candidate wherever MSCP had no candidate.[17] It was also mentioned that there would not be any type of attack and counter attack between FPM and MSCP candidates or party during the election campaign. Federal Party of Manipur also gave an assurance that they would maintain this 'Code of Conduct'. Further they also expressed their desire to work out for, a 'Common Minimum Programme' between the two regional parties under the banner of the 'United Front'. And this plank, according to the desire of the party, should give an ideological commitment on 'Federalism and autonomy'. Thus on the basis of these understanding the two parties agreed to work out a common agenda under the banner of 'United Front.'

In the introductory note of the manifesto the United Front made an appeal to the people of Manipur to give another chance for continuance of their government to complete the unfinished task[18]. It is mentioned that United Front Government had successfully responded to the aspiration of the people of Manipur to have a non-Congress government in the state at the end of the 20th century. To protect the regional interest of Manipur within the framework of Indian nationalism was the basic objective of the United Front Government. They have also mentioned some specific items of works that had been accomplished by the 'United Front Ministry'. They claimed that to bring a successful solution in the Kuki-Zomi clash in Churachandpur was a sincere effort of the government. They further claimed that the successful completion of the National Games in Manipur, the upgradation of Silchar Jiribam railway line into broad gauge, the completion of 36 MW Heavy Fuel Based Power Project at Leimakhong, the 'Loktak Down Stream' project started at a cost of Rs 575 crores, the broadening of National Highway No. 39 and No 53 etc, were some of their accomplished tasks. Along with these works they also put some more agendas for the consideration by the people of Manipur .On the basis of these issues they again requested the people of Manipur for a continuation of their mandate in the election in the 7th Manipur Legislative Assembly 2000 AD[19].

The question of the unity and territorial integrity of Manipur, improvement of law and order situation in the state, autonomy for Manipur, autonomy in the district and village level, social harmony and peaceful resolution of all ethnic social conflicts, negotiation for solution of revolutionary movement, social unity and cultural identity etc, were some important agendas mentioned in the manifesto of the United Front for consideration by the people of Manipur. Apart from these aspects they also made promises to implement some developmental works like, conversion of Manipur University to Central University, improvement of transport and communications, construction of separate hospital for police and security personals, to improve tourism identity, improvement of environment and ecology, fishing project at Loktak, rehabilitation of people affected by Loktak project, polo as a State Game etc. Thus with many promises the United Front requested the people to continue their mandate in favour of them.

In the official statement the president of the party had already spelled out very clearly about the nature of the participation of Federal Party of Manipur in the 7th Manipur Assembly Election. Accordingly the party had fielded up candidates in the 38 Assembly constituencies i.e. 23 in general constituencies and 15 in scheduled tribe assembly constituencies. In some assembly constituencies Federal Party of Manipur and Manipur State Congress Party had sent up their respective candidates and a friendly contest was going between the two parties .In this election Federal Party of Manipur was able to get 6(Six) seats and secured 9.44% of the total vote polled and its 'Front' partner MSCP got 23 (Twenty three) seats and secured 26.28% of the total vote polled .To get 6(Six) seats was a big jump in the political graph of Federal Party of Manipur and it shows that the people of Manipur had warmly received and accepted the ideological principles and objective of the party.

According to the mandate of the people the United Front partners had proposed for the formation of a new ministry. A hectic discussion was going on among the leader of the constituent parties of the 'Front'. Federal Party of Manipur, as a major partner of the 'Front', also makes an attempt to get the ministerial births for all the elected members of the party. The names of the elected members in the 7th Manipur Legislative Assembly were 1) Prof. Gangmumei Kamei from Nungba A/C. 54, 2) Dr. W. Thoiba Singh from Heingang A/C. 2, 3) Dr. L. Bheigyachandra from Keishamthong A/C. 12, 4) Dr. Khasim Ruivah from Chingai A/C 45, 5) Shri Haokholet Kipgen from Saitu A/C 51, 6) K. Raina from Tadubi A/C 49. In a meeting of Federal Legislative Party held on 27th February 2000 AD, the Legislature wing resolved to support the leader of MSCP who was elected by their party. It also further authorized the president of the party to negotiate with the leader of MSCP in respect of ministerial berths and portfolios for the FPM in the new coalition Government[21]. Then the meeting also elected the following MLAs to the respective posts indicated below.

1. Prof. Gangmumei Kamei ——— Leader
2. Dr. W. Thoiba Singh ——— Deputy leader
3. Sheri. Haokholet Kipgen ——— Secretary
4. Dr. L. Bheigyachandra ——— Chief Whip

The resolution of the Federal Legislative Party was forwarded by Prof. N. Joykumar Singh General Secretary to Shri W. Nipamacha Singh President M.S.C.P on the same day .As authorized by the Legislative Party the President of, the party made a sincere effort to accommodate all the MLAs of the party in the ministerial berth. In a confidential letter addressed to Shri. W. Nipamacha Singh, the Chief Minister and leader of MSCP, the President of Federal Party of Manipur had assured him full cooperation to the new ministry headed by MSCP. While giving assurance of support of the party, the President of FPM, by citing the understanding which was made through several consultation on the composition of the next government, had demanded the ministerial positions for all the MLAs of FPM. The ministerial positions as proposed by the party were:-

1.	Prof.Gangmumei Kamei	As a Cabinet Minister at rank No.3 below Deputy CM
2.	Dr. W. Thoiba Singh	To continue as a Cabinet Minister.
3.	Sheri Haokholet Kipgen	As a Cabinet Minister as he is the UF candidate returned from Sardar Hills District (Two times elected).
4.	Dr. Khasim Ruivah	As a Cabinet Minister to represent Ukhrul District as he was the only UF MLA from the District.
5.	Dr. L. Bhagyachandra Singh	Either as a speaker of the Assembly or as a cabinet Minister to represent Imphal urban area.

6. Sheri. K. Raina — As a cabinet Minister as he is the only UF MLA from Senapati area.

He also requested the Chief Minister to allow the six MLAs of FPM to be sworn in as Ministers on the day Chief Minister takes oath.[22]

However all the demands for ministerial posts and positions as expected by the party, was not fully materialized. The party got three cabinet ministers, two state ministers of independent portfolios and Deputy Speaker position. Prof.Gangmumei Kamei, Dr. W. Thoiba Singh, Shri Haokholet Kipgen were in the cabinet position, Dr. Khasim Ruivah , Dr. L. Bhaigyachandra as State Minister and Shri K.Raina as Deputy Speaker. Thus Federal Party of Manipur also had actively participated in the art of the governance of the state as an important partner, of United Front, Ministry.

(G) BYE -ELECTION OF 2000 AD.

The bye-election of Keishamthong Assembly Constituency, which was held in December 2000 A.D, was another remarkable political development of the organizational capabilities of Federal Party of Manipur.The bye-election was held due to the sudden demise of Dr.L. Bhaigyachandra Singh, the State Minister of the Government of Manipur.He was elected from this constituency as a candidate of Federal Party of Manipur. His untimely death had created a sad political situation in the relationship between Federal Party of Manipur and Manipur State Congress Party who were the partners of the United Front Ministry.

However both the parties at the beginning had agreed to send up a common and consensus candidate to contest in this bye–election. From all angles Federal Party of Manipur had a strong privilege to claim for the candidature. It is reported that some top leaders of MSCP were also in favour of the claim of FPM. Then a serious difference of opinion was developed among the rank and files of MSCP and finally they also decided to send up their official candidate. Without having any other alternative both the parties were prepared to have a friendly contest in this bye-election and the FPM selected Shri L. Jayenta Singh, the eldest son of late L. Bheigyachandra Singh to contest the election as their official candidate and MSCP selected Shri. L. Lalit Singh, a former Finance Minister.

Indeed, the nature of election campaign and organizational manoeuvering of FPM in this bye-election was a highly noteworthy and commendable one. All out efforts were made by the party workers under the leadership of Prof.Gangmumei Kamei .The bye –election of Keishamthong assembly constituency was a very big concern for all the media persons and political observers. Because it was a royal election battle for two regional parties who lived together under the same roof of United Front Ministry .On the other hand the MSCP election campaign was led by Shri. W. Nipamacha Singh Chief Minister and Dr. L. Chandramni Singh, Deputy Chief Minister.

In this bye-election the candidate of Federal Party of Manipur was elected by a very big margin. Then the election result gave more strength to the party organisation to expand and consolidate their political activities in the state. It was a remarkable achievement to win the two elections from Keishamthong A/C which is the most educated elitist urban area. Federalism had made a deep indent in urban Manipur.

PARTICIPATION IN THE ELECTION OF LOCAL BODIES.

Apart from the parliamentary and assembly elections the Federal Party of Manipur also actively participated in the elections of various democratic local bodies and political institutions like Municipal Council, Nagar Panchayats etc.As a part of their maiden election participation which was held in the year 1995 the FPM contested in three Municipal councils in the State i.e Imphal Municipal Council, Moirang Municipal Council and Lakshmithongkhong Municipal Council. In Imphal Municipal Council FPM was able to get 2(two) seats, in Moirang Municipal Council 3(three) seats and Laksmithonkhong Nagar Panchayats party got five out of nine seats, Lamshang Nagar Panchayats and Lilong Nagar Panchayats one each.

Thus with the participation in these election the FPM was able to make a successful attempt to expand the organizational activities of the party in every areas of the state and her ideology or objective was also warmly received by the people.

REFERENCES

1. Statement of the FPM in its support to the Congress led ministry.
2. Memorandum submitted by United Democratic Front to the Governor of Manipur.
3. Ibid.
4. President's speech at Federal Working Committee on10th April 1994.
5. The Federal Agenda 1966(The Manifesto of Federal Party of Manipur) p.1
6. Ibid. p.7
7. 'Federal Party and Emergence of the United Front Ministry' A press Release of FPM 24.12. 1997
8. Ibid.
9. Ibid.
10. Ibid.
11. Proceedings of the Working Committee Meeting of FPM held on 9th Dec 1997.
12. Federal Agenda 1999 p.1
13. Ibid.
14. Ibid. p.5
15. Ibid. p.1

16. A statement on the General Election to the 7th Manipur Legislative Assembly by Prof.Gangmumei Kamei, President FPM on 23 rd July 2000 A.D.
17. Ibid.
18. Agenda of United Front, Manipur 2000AD
19. Ibid.
20. Election to the 7th Manipur Legislative Assembly 2000 A.D. list of contested candidate and votes secured.(Directorate of Information and Public Relation, Govt. of Manipur)
21. Proceedings of the meeting of the Federal Legislative Party held on 27th Feb. 2000 AD at 9 a.m at the Official residence of Prof.Gamgmumei Kamei.
22. Confidential letter from Prof. Gangmumei Kamei President of FPM to W. Nipamacha Singh Chief Minister of Manipur and president of MSCP.

CHAPTER FIVE

INVOLVEMENT IN PUBLIC ISSUES

In the framework of democratic process political parties always performed two duties i.e. the participation in the election with an objective to lead the government so that they could translate their agendas into action and to could be able involve in every issues which is directly related in their state and society. This political character was also clearly reflected in the nature of the working of the party. Apart from the participation in the election, the Federal Party of Manipur had also actively involved in many political, economic, social and developmental issues of the State of Manipur. Since federalism and autonomy was the basic ideological principle the party always took a firm political stand for the restructuring of Indian polity. From this fact the Federal Party of Manipur was observed by many social scientists as a local party with a lot of elements of national outlook. The principle of federalism and autonomy itself was an important issue, which involves national interest. Therefore on the basis of this solid ideological foundation the party began to raise some basic issues in the national level. This itself may be treated as a clear manifestation of the contribution of the party in the national political scenario.

POLITICAL

The party started its political involvement in the national mainstream by placing a strong and solid argument for the restructuring of the political system of India. By participating in the debate on the Governor's

Address on the 15th September 1995 Professor Gangmumei Kamei, the president and M.L.A. of the party had strongly demanded to re-examine the role of the Governor as an agent of the ruling party in the system of relationship between of the centre and the state. In a statement which was made inside the Manipur Assembly in connection with the 'Governor's Address'. Prof. Gangmumei Kamei said: -

1 'The Governor's Address is a constitutional requirement. And it is a legal fiction that the Government of State is the Governor's Government. The Governor's Address is a routine affair. What he said and what he did not say is debated in the legislature.

2 However the recent role of the office of the Governor in the trial of strength of the Congress (I) Ministry in involving and flouting the recommendation of the Sarkaria Commission compels us to re-examine the role of the Governor as the agent of the ruling party at the Centre and the State. He has drawn himself in the power game.

3 It also raises the question of the grip of the Centre on the small State of Manipur affecting its autonomy. Manipur was merged with India in1949 and became a member State of Republic of India. Article 2 of the Indian Constitution says that India is a Union of States. The State should have the autonomy, as the present provision is not adequate. Being a Union of State' India should be a federal political structure. Sarkaria Commission highlights the federal structure of the Constitution, federal principle in the Centre and State relation. Does the Governor of Manipur dare to endorse this aspect of the recommendation of the Sarkaria Commission? Would he agree to give more autonomy to the State of Manipur?

4 Federalism implies equal representation of the states in the Federal Parliament of India, which is the Union of States irrespective of population and size. Then it

can accommodate all the diverse elements of a plural society like India.

5 The division of power between the Union and States in the 7th Schedule of the Constitution should be amended. Of the three lists, Union, State and Concurrent, the concurrent list should be abolished. Union list should be limited to Defence, Foreign Affairs, Financial Currency Communication, Federal Legislature; Judiciary and Public Services. The rest should be included in the State list.

6 Article 356 of the Constitution which is an instrument of Central intervention in the State through the Governor should be abolished.

Autonomy for the State of Manipur

7. Manipur was merged with India in 1949. At that time the autonomy and the status of the State were not negotiated but Manipur had its own Constitution known as 'Manipur State Constitution Act 1947' and the Stand Still Agreement respectively to administer her own State and to regulate relation with India. These two documents were not abrogated. The status of Manipur has to be renegotiated and the Pre- Merger State Constitution Act 1947 and the spirit of Article 370(Kashmir) and Article 371(A) autonomy for Nagaland should be made applicable for Manipur also[1]'

Indeed, such type of approach and nature of debate was a new dimension in the character of the working of the Legislative Assembly of Manipur. It laid a foundation for the opening of a new frontier of debate in the thought process among the common people in general and people in the decision making body in particular. This statement gave a new idea among the people particularly on the political issue of the 'Centre State 'relationship.

Again in a letter addressed to Shri H.D.Deve Gowda, the Prime Minister of India, on the 30th June 1996, the party had strongly emphasized the immediate need for the restructuring of Indian polity on the principle of federalism and autonomy for states to fulfill the various ethnic and regional aspirations. For Manipur they demanded the pattern of autonomy which was given to 'Kashmir (Article 370) and Nagaland (Article 371A) and drastic revision of 'Schedule Seven' of the constitution of India which deals with division of powers in the Union List and State List'.[2] They further asserted that the nature of 'Concurrent List' should be applied to Manipur State which was merged into India on 15th October 1949. On the other hand as a responsible political party the F.P.M. also conveyed the support and solidarity of the party to the United Front Government headed by Deve Gowda. The party was of the view that the 'Common Minimum Programme' of the United Front specially on the issue relating to the proposal for the reform in the system of Centre and State relation on the basis of updating the Sarkaria Commission report, reservation of one-third seats in all elected bodies and Government's jobs for women and guarantying 100 days of employment for every unemployed person was definitely a positive stop in the process of political development of the country. Besides, the party also welcomed the idea of the new Government on the issue of the financial autonomy of the State[3].

In the month of October 1997 Shri H.D. Deve Gowda, the Prime Minister of India visited Manipur. At least for Federal Party of Manipur his visit to Manipur was a very significant step towards their process in the political involvement on the national issues. Taking the opportunity of his visit the party again raised the issue for the restructuring of the polity of India in the form of memorandum. In the memorandum submitted to the Prime Minister on the 24th October 1996 the party made a proposal for the establishment of federation and autonomy in Indian polity. In the letter addressed to the Prime Minister of India, the party took the advantage of introducing the Federal Party of Manipur as a 'regional party with a national ideology which emphasized on 'Federation' as the core of Indian political system and autonomy for the state'[4]. At the same time they had also categorically pointed out that one of the basic objective of the party was to get the liberty to enjoy a 'Rightful and Dignified Place' for Manipur in the Indian Republic on the 'Principle of Federalism'[5].

By welcoming the pronouncement of the Prime Minister on the 'Restructure on Indian polity' based on Cooperative Federalism, they also placed the text of the resolutions of the party held on 21st October 1994 in which the issues of 'Federalism and Autonomy for State in Indian Republic was clearly manifested. The detail discussion parts on the resolution of the first convention have already been reflected in the previous chapter. Along with this the party also submitted another memorandum in connection with some burning issues of Manipur. The whole body of the memorandum was constituted by 10 (ten) basic points, which covered almost all the aspects of the state. The demand for the withdrawal of 'Armed Forces Special Power Act 1958', political dialogue between Government of India and revolutionary groups, Law and order situation and corruption in Manipur etc.[6] were the most important features of the memorandum.

In regard to the question of the withdrawal of Armed Forces Special Power Act 1958 the party strongly asserted that "the Armed Forces Special Power Act 1958 has empowered the security forces to trample human rights of the citizens of Manipur who are the subjects in a free and democratic Republic of India. By this Act, the State terrorism has been perpetrated by the state on the people of Manipur. The Act, during the last forty years, had not been able to check or contain insurgency in Manipur." With this solid argument Federal Party of Manipur was of the opinion that the existing laws were sufficient enough to deal with the situation and so the party demanded to withdraw all the 'Black Draconian Laws' from Manipur.

On the question of the political dialogue between the Government of India and revolutionary groups' the party was of the view that the insurgency in Manipur should be tackled at the political level. It was not a mere law and order problem. To developed such type of complex situation in was mainly due to the growth of multiple revolutionary groups with contradictory political objectives operating in the state. Therefore the party asserted that, "the talks should be started without any pre-conditions. In this respect the stand of the party was very clear that any conflict should be settled between the parties concerned keeping in mind the common interest of the people of Manipur. Insurgency in Manipur should be regarded as a national problem, not a local problem."

The party also pointed out the total failure of law and order and practice of rampant corruption in the state. Therefore the Federal Party of Manipur made a proposal to the Prime Minister that an appropriate agency should be constituted by the Union Government to probe the corruptions and scandals in the State of Manipur. At the same time the party also pointed out large scale human right violations, killing of innocent women, men and children and failure to trace out the whereabouts of victim persons who were arrested by the security personnels. The party also urged the Union Government that they should not remained as a helpless spectator[7].

With these views and observations, the president of the party, requested the Prime Minister of India and United Front Government to give a serious thought to the proposal of the party for constitutional change in Indian political system. The memorandum of Federal Party of Manipur was warmly received by the office of the Prime Minister. As a response to the memorandum the Prime Minister wrote a letter to the president of the Party in which he sincerely expressed his strong desire to share the views and ideas of Federal Party of Manipur in the interest of the nation. This development itself was a great achievement in the process of the political involvement of the party.

Then in the year 1997 Shri Indrakumar Gujral, the

Prime minister of India visited the state along with Shri Indrajit Gupta, the Union Home Minister and Union Railway Minister Shri Ram Villas Paswan. Taking the opportunity of their visit the Federal Party of Manipur had submitted a memorandum on the 22nd May 1997. In their memorandum the party again strongly emphasized the immediate need to restructure the Indian polity on the line of the principle of federalism and autonomy for the states. While welcoming the idea of 'Cooperative Federalism' of the Union Government the party vehemently asserted to materialize the principle of federalism that is provided by the Constitution of India.

The Party again reiterated for a dialogue between the Central Government and revolutionary groups without any pre conditions. Indeed this proposal was placed for discussion by the party right from its inception. This proposal was already in the knowledge of the Central Government when Shri Deve Gowda the Prime Minister of India had visited Manipur. As a response to the proposal he himself made an official announcement at Guwahati about the desire of the Central Government to have a dialogue with the insurgents of North East States without any conditions. So to make a convincing positive influence in the process of the policy decision of the Central Government itself was a great achievement on the part of Federal Party of Manipur. Therefore while welcoming the offer of the Government of India to have a dialogue with the different militant outfits of the northeastern region without any conditions, the party, in order to have a smooth sailing in the process of negotiation, had made the following proposal to the Prime Minister as a part of the memorandum. The proposals were: -

1) Necessary grounds for negotiated settlement may be prepared by a 'Group of Persons' of goodwill and knowledge who enjoy the trust of the Government of India, and the revolutionary groups. Such a group may be entrusted by the Government to carry out the task.

2) In order to create a conducive atmosphere for the negotiation, the present military pressure on the militant outfits may be suspended
3) The Armed Forces Special Power Act which gives excessive powers to the Security Forces and which have led to the violation of human rights may be suspended or kept in abeyance
4) The State Governments and various political parties in the region should be taken into confidence before or during the negotiation.[8]

Apart from this the Federal Party of Manipur also had pointed out the chaotic condition in Manipur due to the failure of the Government to contain insurgency, to check corruption, to discipline the police and security forces which have created an atmosphere to violate the human rights and to delay the economic development. The party further mentioned about the existence of two parallel governments in the State i.e., the Government of Manipur and other unseen underground government operating in the valley and hills. The FPM was of the view that the Government had failed to check the parallel government as the ruling party leaders have taken the help of the insurgents for their political purposes. With these observations the Party urged the Prime Minister "to look into this situation to which the government of India has been keeping a Nelson's eye which is a detriment of the nation's interest.[9]

In addition to this the Federal Party of Manipur also proposed for a team of' 'Eminent Citizens for North Eastern Region'. The party was of the view that 'North East Region' was beset with problems some of which were legacy of the colonial past and some are results of the ill informed policies which were implemented by the Government of India. So there was a need to understanding the aspirations of the people of the region and make an attempt to evolve an appropriate solution and mechanism to meet the challenges of the region. The party strongly asserted that the problems of the region should be recognized as a national problem of India and so there was an urgent need to evolve appropriate solution for which some of the best mind of the country should be involved. With these arguments and observations the party asked the Prime Minister to take initiative to persuade eminent citizens and experts of the country to form a team of eminent citizens to make a comprehensive appreciation of the problems of the region and find out the approach to the solution of the complex problem of the region. And such a team if so constituted should have the opportunity to enjoy all required facilities to carry out their mission.[10].

Thus Federal Party of Manipur had successfully involved in the basic political issues of the region as well as nation in particular. On the other hand the idea of federalism and autonomy for states has gradually become a very important issue of every political parties and nation. Every political thinker, social activist and intellectual of India also began to stress the immediate need to restructure the political system for having a secure position of the whole body of Indian Union. From these facts it can be observed that the Federal party of Manipur was also one of the political parties who can influence the thinking process of the central leadership. In this respect the party repeatedly asked its member to understand the real thought and motto of their party. 'Federal Party of Manipur was a local party with a national outlook' was the basic motto of the party. Thus within a short period of time the Federal Party of Manipur was able to play a role of torch bearer on the political issues of state particularly on the principle and federalism and autonomy.

ECONOMIC

Federal Party of Manipur was also fully convinced that the present trend of politics, its approach and thinking is highly influenced by the economic and financial position of the people and state. Prof. Gangmumei Kamei said, 'Economics is the present politics'. It is a known fact that the Federal Party of Manipur was established on the basic foundation of some economic issue of the State of Manipur and its relationship with the Indian Government. The party always regarded Manipur as the market place of the finished products coming from the big industrial houses of the central part of India. To see the financial relationship between the Government of India and Manipur State the party strongly pointed out that instead of self-sufficiency Manipur has become dependent heavily on Central Government. Thus a parasitic culture in the field of economic life was developed in the psychic of the people of Manipur and administration of the state. The role of the State Government was confined purely as a salary-giving agency only. Therefore the only opinion of the party was that under this financial administrative system the economic position of the state could be pulled up only when there was a possibility of self-generating economic condition. This was the basic economic motto of the Federal Party of Manipur. On the basic foundation of this economic concept the party began to involve in many economic issues that was directly or indirectly related with the state.

TENTH FINANCE COMMISSION

The visit of the members of the Tenth Finance Commission in the state under the chairmanship of Shri K.C.Pant was a major break through of the Federal Party of Manipur in their conceptual framework of economic policy. Taking the advantage of their visit the party was able to highlight the present economic issues of the state and placed the ways and means that was considered by the party as an alternative for the improvement of financial conditions of Manipur. Therefore the party had prepared well in advance for a proposal for the improvement of the financial conditions of the state. Dr. Amar Yumnam the Economic Advisor to the Federal Party of Manipur was the main architect of the economic policy of the party. In order to place the views of the party he, in consultation with other party leaders had prepared the memorandum on the line of the economic concept of the party. The party called it as 'ECONOMIC BLUE PRINT FOR REGENERATION OF MANIPUR'. The president of the Party had submitted the memorandum on the 8th April 1994.

The whole body of the memorandum is divided into eight parts including the introduction. In the introductory part the Federal Party of Manipur gave a positive observation about the New Economic Policy (NEP) of the Government of India. The essence of economic competition into the Indian economy was warmly welcomed and supported by the party and regarded it as a definitely welcome change. The party thought that the implication of 'New Economic Policy' was to give an opportunity to every state to fend for them by generating their own financial position. Indeed this was an outcome of the failure of the earlier planning efforts to lay any foundation for a sustained and long run development. The basic objective of NEP was to make a competition among the states in the play of the marked forces. That possibility was not in the case of Manipur as the earlier planning did not make any effort to establish a field of comparative advantage. The party was of the view that a tendency to sustain the economic growth and development would be existed if a comparative advantage in a field once established. This was not in the case of Manipur because all the earlier planning efforts had failed to surpass the hurdles of zero sum attitudes and to generate positive sum attitude instead. The memorandum also pointed out the results of the earlier planned efforts. The results were: -

a) Generation of rent seeking behavior as evidenced by the prevalence of widespread corruption in the state and

b) Emergence of only unproductive and destructive entrepreneurs rather than productive entrepreneurs as evidenced by the widespread prevalence of lottery culture and emergence of anti social elements.[11]

The memorandum further mentioned that the immediate impact of the result of the above-mentioned factor is that "the consumption possibilities frontier has been expanded without a corresponding expansion of the production possibilities frontier. This has created a fundamental imbalance in the economy with far reaching implications for economy, society and finance of the state". [12] On the basis of this fact the Federal Party of Manipur was of the view that the only remedy to the ailing economy and to bring about a background and sustained development in the state was to adopt a 'big push' policy. The party strongly felt that to establish and ensure a comparative advantage in the field of economy the state requires a huge 'one time investment'.

The party also pointed out three important major factors that create a serious financial problem in the state. They were: -

1. Unestablishment of foundation for a sustained development in the state.
2. Over burdened with interest and loan repayment liabilities faced by the state.
3. Limited scope in the state for further for resource mobilization [13]

In addition to this the memorandum also highlighted a serious financial problems created by interest liabilities of the states. By giving a statistical figure of nine years i.e. from 1984-1985 to 1992-1993 the party had pointed out of the fact that the state has been spending on an average Rs. 80 to 90 crores annually for capital repayments. If the loan payment and interest was combined it could be seen that an average the state spend more than 20% of each annual expenditure on interest and loan adjustment only. This was really an unhealthy financial atmosphere so far the developmental work of the state is concerned on the following grounds. They were:-

1. The level of the development of the state is very low already;
2. The size of the state's budget is not a big one and can in any way provide a big push;
3. The earlier expenses had failed to provide a production base for the state's economy and create an atmosphere for the emergence of productive entrepreneur and
4. in the above circumstances , spending of more than 20% of the state expenditure on interest and loan repayments can only stunt the growth possibilities of the state further[14].

In regard to the scope for Additional Resource Mobilization (ARM) the party was of the view that though the 'New Economic Policy' asked the states to generate their own resources to meet any further expenses it would not be possible in the case of Manipur because the scope for Additional Resource Mobilization (ARM) was already shrinking and so there would not be any improvement in the given economic heritage of the state.

After analyzing all the financial and economic condition of the state the Federal party of Manipur had categorically pointed out that what the state required was a big push immediately to ensure a sustained growth in the long run. The fact was that the state has no production base and no scope for Additional Resource Mobilization.(ARM) . With these arguments the party by giving the present economic conditions of Manipur made a proposal to provide a sum of Rs.6, 500/- cores (Six thousand five hundred cores) for the development of the state for extending facilities to regenerate the economic condition. The items were:-

SL. NO.	ITEM	CRORES
1.	Infrastructure, specially, roads and communications in the hill areas	1,500.00
2.	Agriculture and Horticulture	2,000.00
3.	Rehabilitation of the people affected by the recent alteration	100.00
4.	Police Hospital	400.00
5.	Imphal City Complex	1,000.00
6.	District headquarters Town	500.00
7.	Development of Loktak and its surrounding areas	1,000.00
	Grand Total	**65000.00**

(Six thousand five hundred crores)

The spirit of the memorandum and its style of approach were received warmly by the members of the Finance Committee headed by K.C. Pant. The party was represented by three members. They were Prof. Gangmumei Kamei, President, Dr. N. Joykumar Singh, General Secretary and Shri M. Maringa, Vice President. The chairman of the Finance Commission gave a reasonably enough time to the party for having a detailed discussion on the proposal of the memorandum. The idea of the provision of 'economic package of Federal party of Manipur was welcomed by every member of the Finance Committee. On the line of the proposal of FPM the Government of India immediately provided a large amount of money for the development of the entire areas of North Eastern Region. Therefore the ideas and policies, which were reflected in the memorandum, was a great contribution of the FPM in the process of the economic development of the State. On the other hand it was also a unique involvement of the party in the process of the regeneration of the Financial position of the state of Manipur.

ELEVENTH FINANCE COMMISSION

In May 1999 a team of 'Eleventh Finance Commission' visited Manipur to discuss the financial issues of the state. All the political parties and social organizations were invited by the state government to meet the members of the commission. Taking this opportunity FPM also submitted a memorandum on 19th May 1999. The nature of the argument of FPM was slightly different from the approach of the memorandum of the Tenth Finance Commission. In the meeting the party was represented by Prof. N. Joykumar Singh General Secreatary and Dr. Amar Yumnam , Economic Advisor of the party. The chairman of the Eleventh Finance Commission was Prof. Khusru an eminent economist of international stature.

At the very outset the party expressed their reservation on the nature of their approach. By pointing out the basic objectives of the Finance Commission i.e. (a) to restore financial equilibrium of the state and (b) to establish horizontal and vertical balance of the finance of the state, the party said that all the Finance Commission so far have erred in viewing the states mainly as population units rather then as economic units. The nature of such approach was regarded by the party as a work against the interest of small states like Manipur despite the apparent case expressed for them[15]. The approach of the argument of the party was that almost 80% or so of the devolutions had been on the basis of population so far. By giving the justification of this argument the party said;

"First there is the usual share calculated on the basis of size of population of a census. Besides while calculating the devolution on the basis of per capita income, there is an in a built element of population, which makes the devolution of the state with big population economically handsome and that to a state with small population economically meaningless. The devolution on the basis of these two calculations has always constituted 80 % of the total. So, the share of the state with population of big size has always been substantive in absolute terms and *ipso facto*, meaningful financially and economically. In other words, whatever meaningful seen could be expected by the state of small population size was for the remaining 20% of the divisible period. This implies that the devolution granted to these states have been compiled with the small size of plan investment also in absolute term, in these later states, thereby forever reducing or stunting the economic feasibility of these"[16].

The party also pointed out another disadvantageous position faced by the small states like Manipur so far their financial development matter was concerned. It mentioned that since most of the private domestic investments so far have taken place in the state with large population, the small states were not able to get the facilities from these financial agencies. Therefore the party proposed to provide financial facilities on the basis of the population should be corrected and in order to have a financial equilibrium among the states the provision of the financial distribution should be made on the basis of economic units. On the basic agreement of this direction FPM proposed that 50% of the total devolution should be made on population related variable and another 50% on economic related variable[17].

After giving a general arguments and observations the party gave characteristic features of the existing economic position of the State of Manipur. The memorandum had mentioned four aspects as the main factors of the existing economic position. They were: -

1. Increasing dichotomy between consumption and production, both in the quality and composition.
2. Weak production base and *ipso facto*, very little scope for additional resource mobilization
3. Increasing indebtedness, and thereby near complete topsy-turvy of the planning process and

4. Budgetary subsidization of the State Public Sector Understanding (SPSU) [18]

The memorandum also gives a detail explanation of these features. Thus after giving an exhaustive observations and explanation the Federal Party of Manipur requested the Commission to extend to the state the following financial assistance with a view to giving a big push to the economy:

Sl. No.	ITEMS	AMOUNT (CRORE)
1.	Debt clearing	600.00
2.	One time grant to SPSUS	500.00
3.	Infrastructure, Specially Roads & communication in the hill area, while at the same time addressing Environmental issues.	2000.00
4.	Agriculture and Horticulture	1500.00
5.	Establishment of tea Estates in Tamenglong, Senapati and Ukhrul areas of the state	200.00
6.	Police Hospital	400.00
7.	One time Grant to Manipur University	40.00
	Grand Total	**5240.00**

(Five thousand two hundred fifty crores)

The arguments in general conceptual issues about the nature of the devolution and areas of financial requirements printed out in the memorandum were highly appreciated in the course of the deliberation. Even the members of the Commission said that it was a new approach of argument and an important issue. Thus the FPM had greatly involved in the economic life of the state by giving a basic strong foundation for financial concept, which is the most important vision for any type of economic development.

Apart from the Financial Commission, the party also makes a various attempt for the positive economic development in the state by requesting the Central Government. The announcement of special economic package for the North Eastern Region by Shri Deve Gowda, the Prime Minister of India in the year 1996, was treated by the party as a positive direction in the process of the possibilities of self- generating economic condition of the small states in this region. This was also an economic thesis of the party. Under this special economic package the United Front Government had announced seven projects for Manipur. While appreciating the announcement of the Central Government the FPM urged the authority to implement the package, which would go a long in bringing a positive transformation in the economy of the state. Along with this the party also requested the Central Government to continue the policy of Basic Minimum Service (BMS) in the subsequent years. The party was of the opinion that this would give a new economic hope to the people of the isolated far filing areas of Manipur who have been neglected for years[19]

Thus as a state based political party the FPM with limited jurisdiction also played a significant role for the economic prosperity of the state. Indeed, the basic economic philosophy which was placed by the party in the 10th and 11th Finance Commissions would be the guiding principle for having the opportunely for the self generating economic condition of Manipur.

SOCIAL AND DEVELOPMENTAL ISSUES

Besides, political and economic aspects FPM also had actively involved in many social and developmental issue of the state. The principle of social equilibrium is the basic motto of the party. On this basic point the party had introduced the idea of 'social federalism' with an objective to maintain peace and harmony among the ethnic groups of people. Another aspect was to promote development with social justice. The equitable economic development was the basic principle of the party in relation to the developmental programme of the state. But these issues, which had already been mentioned above, would not be possible to implement very successful without financial involvement. Since the state had an acute financial position any type of developmental works was not able to take up properly. Therefore the involvement of the Central Government was highly needed for this purpose. Keeping this view into consideration FPM took up the issues of the developmental aspect of the state. This was also the view of the party that the development of the state could be possible only with the assignment of Central Government. Accordingly a series of representation was made by the party in the form of memorandum. Most of them were addressed to the Prime Minister of India.

In a memorandum submitted to Shri H.D.Deve Gouda the Prime Minister of India the FPM demanded to implement the following schemes.

1. Implementation of Special Employment Scheme in Manipur to make the unemployed problems among the educated youths.
2. Conversion of the N.H. 53 into double lane and all weather roads.
3. Conversion of Manipur University into Central a Central University.
4. Railway connection to Manipur
5. A Circular State High way like all the District Headquaters.
6. A regional Engineering college for Manipur
7. Massive involvement for horticulture development in the hills and irrigation facilities for the facilities for the plains of Manipur.
8. Central finance for Loktak Downstream Hydro Project.
9. Facility for local entrepreneurs in the Indo Myanmar trade
10. Massive investment in the development and management of the Loktak lake solution of the

problem of inundation on large track of agricultural land by the Ithai barrage[20].

In addition to this the party also asked the Central Government for the immediate completion of the process of shifting of the Assam Rifles from Kangla Fort to the new site allotted to them by the State Government.[21].

In a memorandum submitted to Shri Atal Behari Vajpayee, the Prime Minister of India when he visited Manipur in May 1999, Federal Party of Manipur, apart from the economic issues like plan financing, the debts of the state, to provide one time financial investment etc, had strongly emphasized to give more attention to the development of the state. At that time the Central Government had conceived an idea to construct a "National Super Highway Project" to integrate the national economy FPM also warmly welcomed this project as a genuine necessity for national economic integration. Taking the advantage of the situation and realising the economic potential of the project, the party made an appeal to the Prime Minister in the form of a memorandum to extend this project up to Moreh in Manipur for doing justice to a state which have been by-passed by the railways[22] .The party also believed that the working and sense of the feeling of the existence of the government should be made available in the minds of the people to the remote, hill and inaccessible areas of the state. It is felt that this could be possible only with the improvement of the means of the road communications. Therefore in order to have one more communications line with the other parts of the neighboring state, in addition to National Highway No. 39 and 53 the party also asked the Central Government to complete National Highway No 150 and made operational at the earliest[24]

Federal Party of Manipur also had fully convinced that the development of the state towards the positive direction would be possible only when the social and economic condition of the peasant and farmers and other down trodden people were improved. Therefore as a responsible political party FPM also had made a separate platform which have the sole Federal authority to look into and to discuss the issue of the peasant and farmer of Manipur. It was known as 'Federal Pwasant Front'. The party also believed that 'Manipur could be save only when the society promote and foster the suppress peasant of valley and hills who constitute 80% of the total population of the State. The development of Manipur lies on the prosperity of peasant and farmers. The responsibilities of the proper functioning of the Peasant Front of the party were assigned to Shri Brajamani Thoudam a devoted and sincere social worker. Under his presidentship the party had submitted a memorandum consisting of 20(twenty) points to Shri W. Nipamacha Singh, the Chief Minister of Manipur on 20th June 2000 A.D. Some of the important issues raised by the Peasant Front of the party were: -

A. to give reasonable subsidies to the peasant on fertilizer

B. to introduce "seed policy" in the state in order to get good quality of seeds.

C. to provide irrigation and water facilities throughout the year

D. to introduce "National Agricultural Insurance Scheme"in order to make it as a remedy to the peasant against the destruction of food grain by natural calamities like flood, draught and insecticides

E. to observed the 30th June as a" Peasant Day' annually, etc.

In a memorandum submitted to Shri Nitish Kumar, the Union Minister of Agriculture the Federal Party of Manipur urged the Central Government to increase the subsidy of Rs. 30,000/- (Thirty thousand), which have been given by the Government of India to small and marginal farmers to purchase small tractors up to 30 H.P. under Farm Mechanization Scheme, which was a centrally sponsored scheme. The justification of the party was that the farmers of North Eastern Region particularly Manipur was very poor and nationalized banks operating in Manipur were very much reluctant to advance loans to farmers, as they feared that since the farmers were poor they would not be able to pay loans. Under this circumstance the farmers of this state would not be in a position to purchase tractors costing Rs, 3 lakhs or more per tractor. Therefore the party urged him to increase the subsidy rates to rupees one lakh per tractor. Apart from this the party also asked the Union Agricultural Minister to implement the 'Crop Insurance Scheme' which had not been implemented so far in Manipur and to take up a scheme for rehabilitation of displaced peasants by Loktak Hydro Electric Project.[24]

In the year 1997 the party also submitted a memorandum to Shri Charan Singh, Chairman Parliamentary Standing Committee on Agriculture in which the party requested the Central Government to provide the following facilities in Manipur They were

a. Irrigation facilities
b. Alternative agricultural land to the effected farmers by Loktak Hydro electric project
c. Massive horticultural facilities to the hill areas
d. Facilities of agricultural education to the farmers
e. Tea cultivation as a means and facilities and as an innovation scheme[25].

Thus FPM right from the very inception had actively participated and involved in every political, economic and developmental issues of the state. It is also worthy to note that the issue raise by the party particularly on the question of the restructuring of Indian political system has become a great concerned for every political parties and the matter was seriously discussed among the intellectuals of India. The idea of an economic package initiated by the Federal Party of Manipur was treated by the Union Government as a national policy. This was a great contributory achievement of the party. With this involvement the party had successfully played a value base politics in the state in particular and national in general.

REFERENCES

1. "STATEMENT ON GOVERNOR'S ADDRESS" A written speech of Prof.Gangmumei Kamei, M.L.A. in the Manipur Legislative Assembly on 15. 9. 95 (Reproduced).
2. Letter from Prof.Gangmumei Kamei President of FPM to Shri H.D Deve Gowda the Prime Minister of India on 30th June 1996.
3. Ibid.
4. "A PROPOSAL FOR FEDERALISM AND AUTONOMY IN INDIAN POLITY" (A Memmorandam submitted to Shri H.D Deve Gowda, the Hon'ble Prime Minister of India. Imphal 24th October 1996.
5. Ibid.
6. Memorandam submitted to Shri H.D Deve Gowda Hon'rable Prime Minister of India Imphal 24th October 1996.
7. Ibid.
8. Memorandam submitted to Shri I.K. Gujral, Hon'ble Prime Minister of India. Imphal 22nd May 1998.
9. Ibid.
10. Ibid.
11. 'A BUUEPRINT FOR ECONOMIC REGENERATION OF MANIPUR' Memorandum submitted to the Tenth Finance Commission Imphal April 8,1994 p.1
12. Ibid.
13. Ibid. p.2
14. Ibid. p.3
15. Memorandum Submitted to the Eleventh Finance Commission by Federal Party of Manipur. p.1
16. Ibid.
17. Ibid.
18. Ibid. p.3

19. Memorandam submitted to Shri Inder Kumar Gujaral, The Hon'ble Prime Minister of India, 22nd May 1997 p.1.
20. Memorandam submitted to Shri H.D Deve Gowda, The Prime Minister of India, and 24th October 1996. pp. 4-5
21. Ibid. P 2
22. Memorandum submitted to Shri Attal Behari Vajpayee the Prime Minister of India. 20th May 1999. p. 2
23. Ibid.
24. Memorandum submitted to Shri Nitish Kumar Union Minister of Agriculture by Sri Brajamani Thoudam, President Federal Peasant Front, FPM dated 13-9-2000.
25. Memorandum submitted to Shri. Siva Charan Dev, Chairman Parliamentary Study Committee on Agriculture by Federal Party of Manipur. 9th June 1997.

CHAPTER SIX

NEW FRONTRUNNER

The last part of 2000 A.D was a very significant period of Federal Party of Manipur in her ongoing process of political activities. It was a transition period of the political activities of the party between the old and the new leadership. This new political development in the party particularly in the change of leadership was an indirect outcome of the result of the internal crisis in the 'United Front Ministry'. At that time a serious internal political crisis was developed particularly among the rank and file of the leadership of Manipur State Congress Party, the major political partner and the leader of the 'United Front Ministry'. The issues were more or less directly related with the demand of the change of leadership in the legislature wing of the party. This issue had created an undesirable political scene and produced some kind of instability among the members of the legislative members of the 'Front' and ultimately it effects the normal functioning of the government. In course of time, though it was not in an apparent way groupism was developed inside the 'Front'. 'Federal Party' of Manipur became the first victim under this new political game of groupism.

Taking the advantage of this new crisis inside the 'Front Ministry' the other political leaders who were the aspirant for chief Ministership attempted to win over the support of members of the legislative assembly of the 'Front'. Federal Party of Manipur became the first soft target of their attack and they were able to get the support of two M.L.A's of this party. They were Shri Haokholet Kipgen of Saitu (ST) Assembly Constituency and L. Jayenta Singh of Keishamthong Assembly constituency. Indeed, the defection of two M.L.As was a great unprecedented jolt to Federal Party of Manipur. As has already been mentioned above about the main objective for the establishment of Federal Party of Manipur as a state based political party. There was a wide range positive response to the objectives and agendas from the masses and to see such a good response an impression was developed among the leadership of the party that Federal Party of Manipur would be able to materialize their objectives and agendas without any disturbances in their political activities. Though the defection was a part of the political life of other political parties in Manipur but for FPM it was a new experience. Since most of the leadership of the party had little experience of this politics of defection it gave serious setback in the functioning of party organization.

In the meantime the degree of the internal crisis in the 'United Front Ministry' had reached in a more and more deeper stage and ultimately Federal Party of Manipur was compelled by the situation to withdraw from the 'Front' ministry'. While this was the situation Shri Radhabinod Koijam of Samata Party had claimed the majority support of M.L.As and demanded to form a new ministry under his leadership. He formed a new legislature group known as 'People's Front'. This was a very delicate situation of the party particularly in their nature of political decision. The party was of the view that if the present trend of political situation continued furthers the degree of the possibilities of the direct interference of the Central Government would be very high. Such type of political development itself was against basic political stand of the party. From the very inception the party's political stand was against any type of direct interference of Central Government in the process of the democratic functioning of the State Government. Therefore they strongly claimed for the abrogation of the Art.356 of the Indian Constitution which provides room for direct interference of Central Government in the functioning of the State Government. Accordingly an issue was developed before the leaders on the question whether the party should support the new ministry or not. While this was the situation the leader of the 'People Front' also invited the FPM to join the new coalition government. Accordingly on 14th February 2001 a joint meeting of Federal Legislature Party and office bearers of the organization was held at the office of the party. The members who were present at the meeting were:-Prof. Gangmumei Kamei (President) M.L.A, W. Thoiba Singh M.L.A, Dr. Khasim Ruivah M.L.A, Shri. K. Raina M.L.A, Shri L.Jayentakumar Singh, Vice President, Prof. N. Joykumar Singh General Secretary, Shri. S. Brajagopal Sharma General Secretary.[1] The focus point of their discussion was concentrated on the issue whether they should stand for the promotion and safeguarding of democratic institution or not. There was a sharp difference of opinion between the members of legislature and organisation wings. The MLAs were in favour of joining the new Ministry and members were not in favour of it. The opinion of the office bearers was based on the ground reality. After having a detail discussion the meeting came to a conclusion that since Federal Party of Manipur, stands for the basic democratic right of the people they should not encourage any type of political decision which might affect the essence of democracy. On the other hand the party also strongly demanded to abrogate the Art.356 of Indian constitution which the party always considered as a weapon for the murder of democracy. Keeping these views into considerations and to promote the democratic principles the Federal Party of Manipur had finally decided to join the new ministry headed by Shri Radhabinod Koijam.

However, within a very short period of time the party

again faced another political development of the defection of two more M.L.As. 1. Dr. W. Thoiba Singh and Shri. K. Raina. Their defection from the party had produced a serious negative impact in the nature of the working of the party. On the other hand, this new trend of political development had produced an atmosphere to question the integrity, maturity and capabilities of the present leadership. To see all these undesirable political situations and to check the deteriorating conditions in the organization the leadership of the party placed several issues for discussion. The issues were coined as 'Task Before Us' and it includes seven points. They were:-

1. FPM is facing crisis due to the defection of 4 M.L.As.
2. FPM is a partner in the present People's Front Government lead by Shri. Radhabinod Koijam. Should we continue this partnership or withdraw from the 'Ministry' and be in the opposition?
3. FPM has withstood the pressure from other party and maintains our identity.
4. FPM has confidence in the present leadership? If not should we change the leadership.
5. FPM is fairly committed to federalism and autonomy. Should we go to the grass root of the society and mobilize the support of the masses.
6. FPM has to build a solid organization base: Trained workers are needed for all fouls.
7. FPM should form its core group, a think tank or old party elders"[2]

It was a very important meeting that it again laid a basic foundation for the revitalization of the political activities of the party with a clear political stand and distinctive identity. Accordingly all the party workers had proposed to face any type of challenge, which might have come from any type of political situation. Federal Party withdrew from the Radhabinod ministry and joined the Democratic People's Alliance to form and the ministry. This move was rejected by the NDA government. As no ministry could be formed, the Assembly was suspended and President's Rule was imposed on 2nd June 2001.

On June 14 2001 the Government of India and NSCN (IM) made an agreement to extend the Indo-Naga Ceasefire without territorial limits. This new development was a serious contradiction to the basic stand of Federal Party of Manipur on the question of the territory of Manipur. Right from the very inception the political stand of the party in this very issue was very cleared. Their opinion was that at no point of their discussion the question of the boundary of the state of Manipur and extension of ceasefire between NSCN (IM) and Government of India into her territory should be figured. The view of the party was that Manipur is a historically evolved state and she merged into the political boundary of Indian union with an agreement. Therefore it was an obligatory on the part of the Indian government to pay respect the spirit of the agreement and distinctive historical identity of this place. The basic objective of the party on this issue was that since the merger agreement had respected the present areas as the boundary of Manipur it is an obligations on the part of the Government of India to pay proper attention and respect to the status quo of the agreement. Federal Party of Manipur was against any type of political development which may lead for the disturbances of cultural and territorial identity of Manipur. Therefore when the issue for extension of ceasefire was developed the FPM also immediately reacted to the decision of the government of India

The extension of ceasefire into the territory of Manipur become a very hot issue in their social and political life of the state. It sparked the minds of the people of Manipur. Finally it caused for an outburst on the 18th June. A serious turmoil was erupted in the capital of Manipur and flames of anger of the people were occurred everywhere in different forms. Assembly building was burnt and completely destroyed and almost many official quarters of M.L.A s were attacked and burnt down. The

Raj Bhavan,Chief Minister's Security were also attacked. On that day many people become the victim of this issue. However due to the objection and protest of the people and the PIPs and MlLAs Forum of Manipur, the Naga – India ceasefire was rolled back from Manipur on 27th july,2001.

Federal Party of Manipur also began to play the role of an effective opposition political party. At the same time they also tried to improve the working of the organization. Prof. Gangmumei Kamei expressed his desire for a change of leadership in view of the ethnic tension in Manipur. But nobody was ready to take the responsibilities of the leadership of the party. Thus the party working was continued for sometime without any activities. This was a turning point in the whole political life of Federal Party of Manipur.

In the meantime there were a lot of new political polarizations among the members of these political parties. The Manipur State Congress Party was the biggest victim in the process of this new polarization. The party was divided into three groups. A big group led by Dr. L. Chandramni Singh came out from the party and prepared either to establish a new political party or to join hand with other regional or national level political parties. While this was the situation a new political understanding was established between FPM leadership with the group of Dr. L. Chandramni Singh. Ultimately they had decided to join the Federal Party of Manipur. Thus with the coming of the large chunk of people from MSCP had produced changes in the nature of the character of the Federal party of Manipur.

To negotiate the formal joining the MSCP breakaway groups of Ex MLAs led by Dr. Chandramani. FPM had constituted a 'Political Affairs Committee' of five memberships under the chairmanship of Prof. N. Joykumar Singh. The other members were Shri Maringa, Dr. N. Sarat Singh, Shri. Brajagopal Sharma and Shri L. Memo Singh. On 25th September 2001 A.D a joint meeting was held between the committee of FPM and group of Chandramni Singh's supports. The committee members of this group were Shri M. Kunjo Singh . Dr. W. Thoiba Singh, Shri. M. Kumar Singh and Shri. L. Tomba Singh. In this meeting the two committee discussed the terms and conditions for a final process. In the meantime Prof. Gangmumei Kamei, the President of FPM had offered his resignation from the president. Then on 4th October 2001 the General Body meeting of the party was convened at Majorkhul Community hall. Certain amendment was made in the provision of the constitution of the party by this meeting by exercising the power given in the constitution. Under that changing provision the meeting elected Dr. L. Chandramni Singh unanimously as the next president of Federal Party of Manipur. Prof. Gangmumei Kamei: the founder President handed over the reign of the party to the new incumbent.

The immediate task before the new president was how to carry the party in the coming general election of 2002 A.D. It was a big test for him. Like the previous election patterns, in this election also the Federal Party of Manipur sent up candidate in 48 assembly constituencies. The election campaign was made under the slogan of 'New United and Prosperous Manipur'. They also claimed that since the basic political of Indian democracy and federal structure is based on federalism and federal structure the principles of this political concept should also be made practicable in the relationship between Centre or State. In this election also the party strongly emphasized the immediate need of federal spirit in the Indian democracy. The Supreme Court of India and Inter State Council also admitted this idea and it was also reflected in Indian constitution itself. Even the Constitution Review Commission also has given thought on the Centre State relation and autonomy for states. However the Federal Party of Manipur, right from the beginning had an impression that the political attitude of the Central Government was always under the control of the 'hegemonic and centralist forces forces representing the upper class of higher caste of mainland' India. In this election also the party strongly reiterated her firm commitment to federalism, autonomy and regionalism within the Indian nationalism and also made a solemn pledge to the people of Manipur to secure for this united ancient state a rightful and dignified place in the Republic of India.

The result of the general election was quite encouraging. She was able to secure 13(thirteen) seats. The graph in the number game was quite favourable to the party. The first count of the election game was only two then to six and in the election of 2002 A.D the figure increased to thirteen. From this fact the result of the election was a triumph of the issues and agendas placed by the party for the welfare of the people.

However change of leadership had produced a far reaching impact in the nature of the style of working of the party. The concept of the collective leadership which was established from the very inception was seriously eroded. The introduction of inter-party bureaucracy in the rank and file of the membership has widened the gap of understanding and close relationship between party workers and leaders. Due to this new development the workers were not able to understand fully the policy and programe of the party leadership. As a result of this absence of transparency in the functioning of the party a serious problem of the lack of the confidence was developed in the relationship between workers and leaders.

Another new development was the ignorance of the party leadership of the basic issues of the state and lack of commitment to the ideology and agendas of the party. It is a known fact that in the graph of the electoral politics the party was able to get a respectable position by securing the 13(thirteen) seats. However, due to the non- committal working style of the leadership the importance of the party was gradually diminished from the minds of the common people. This factor might be caused mainly due to the lack of clear vision about the priority in the mindset of the leadership of the party. The leadership was of the view the effective working system in the party could be possible only when the party was in power. And so they were of the view that organisation activities would be able to strengthen only after the formation of ministry. Therefore under this inner idea the party leaders devoted their time and energy in an unsuccessful attempt for the formation of a government. On the other hand this concept brought about a serious havoc in the functioning of the party organisation.

So far as the working style is concerned this new system was quite contradictory from the earlier practices. The idea of collective leadership is clearly reflected in the earlier working system. Each and every member had an impression in their minds that they were all answererable to the party. Therefore without any exception every member tried to discharge their assigned duties very effectively. Because of this reason, though the position and strength of the party was in a negligible status in the political arena of the state, the members were able to campaign very effectively for the promotion of the idea and principle in every nook and corner of Manipur. A consisitent type of political activities was carried on by the party by involving in every social, economic and political issues of the state.

On the other hand due to the lack of interest in the working of the organisation the importance and value of the party was also not clearly reflected in the minds of the elected members (MLA) of the party. Therefore a gap of understanding was developed between organisation and elected members. Whatever the case it may be but if the totality of all the political activities of the party is to be studied it can be said that just after the change of leadership the value of the party and confidence which were in the minds of the common people was diminished. There was an impression among the minds of the party workers that the party might have been merged with another state political party, but it was not materialised. Perhaps a serious objection might be there from other leaders. The basic slogans of autonomy and federalism are no more heard. Formation of coalition government proceeded in the organizational development. The only mentioned statement that party organisation after capture of power had demoralized the rank and file of the party. Therefore such type of serious departure in the nature of the working style of new leadership has produced a serious repurcussion in the organizational functionary of the party. The less involvement in every issue of the people and state in general has laid a foundation for the raise of so many questions on the sincerity and wisdom of the party particularly in their ideology, agendas and even the basic principle of their commitment to the cause of the people. Looking from different angles it can be observed that the change of leadership has not produced a desire result for the strengthening of the working of the organisation. However, some important leaders expressed that Federal Party of Manipur will march to a future glory in course of time.

REFERENCES

1. Proceedings of the meeting of the Legislature Party of FPM held on 14th Feb.2001.
2. 'Task before Us' an issue paper of the party circulated for general discussion on 14.3.2001

CHAPTER SEVEN
CONCLUSION

A political party is a public platform established by a like-minded group of people with an objective to promote and foster the national interest within the framework of some specific agendas and ideological principles. The importance of the political party and its role was not in existence at a particular period of time when the autocratic and dictatorial regimes were in full practice in every state and society .It is mentioned that the concept of the term political party was emerged with the development of representative institutions and expansion of the system of suffrage It is also a fact that the growth of the idea of equality and liberty among the people are the basic foundation for the birth of the principle of democracy. And these principles are the basis for the organisation of political parties. The importance of the existence and value of the functioning of political parties provided only in the state where the principles of democratic policy is fully established.

Under the democratic norms the governance of a state is to be performed through a collective wisdom of the political parties. Edmunf Burk said, 'political party is a body of men united for promoting by their joint endeavor the national interest upon some particular principles in which they are agreed.' Gilchrist was of the view that 'a political party may thus be defined as an organised group of citizens who prefers to share the same political views and who by acting as political unit, try to control the government.' It is also mentioned "a political party, in a free society, is an organised group of citizens having the purpose of controlling the government through shared consent, by placing some of its members in public office". Some writers are of the view that "political party is an autonomous, organised group that makes nominations and contests election in the hope of eventually getting and exercising control of the personnel and policies of the government". Since the principle of rule by the majority is the essence of the democracy, the mandate of the people is the basic framework of the governance of the state. Therefore one of the basic objectives of a political party is to control the legislature and to influence over the policies of the government by enforcing their views and objectives. To control legislature under the democratic principles means to get majority in the number game of the elected bodies. From this point of view it can be suggested that another feature of the party, besides their agendas and objectives, is to manage election to get more members in their command. In fact, political party is an indispensable feature of democratic institutions and system is fully determined only by the positive performance of the political parties of the given state.

Political parties are established due to many determinant factors. However according to Alan K. Ball, political party is established broadly by three important factors i.e. historical, socio-economic and ideological. He was of the view that 'parties arise when historical changes occur'. As has already been mentioned above about the importance of political parties in the governance of the state, that since the democratic system and principle have become a prerequisite factor in the modern political scenario, the political parties has taken a very important role as a creation of modern political process. Therefore the establishment of a political party is closely related with changing historical process of the society. The growth of new political consciousness and issue among the masses is made possible only through the platform of the political parties. The establishment of a political party is closely related with changing historical process of the society. The growth of new political consciousness and idea among the masses is made possible only through the plateform of the political parties. The establishment of various political parties in the world was closely related with changing historical development of the state and society. The birth of political parties in Europe particularly in England was closely influenced by the changing historical process. The birth of Congress Party in India was directly related with changing historical development of the country. Therefore historical factor is an important determinant cause for the birth of a political party.

Changing historical process is the direct influence of the growing social and economic development in the given state. It is a known fact that human mind is not at all static and they are always look forward for the development of their social and economic life. At the same time they are also involved in this changing process. These new ideas of economic development, particularly in the state, where the democratic system is fully in operation given a very important room for a healthy competition among the political parties. The class conflict, the different economic and social life between urban and rural areas, the idea of nationalism, sectarian outlook based on religious believe etc. are the important factors for the birth of different political parties. Apart from the national level political parties, the birth of regional and local base political party particularly in the context of India, is mainly due to the different economic and social factors which are now prevailing in different regions of the country.

The idea of how a political party has a relationship with the existing political system could be seen only through their ideological principles. The ideology of political party is closely connected with existing social and economic life of the society. Therefore political party is established on the basis of the prevailing social and economic process of the country. The basis of the emergence of socialist ideological parties was the outcome of the growing economic changes and its impact on the class relationship among the people in the society. It is a well aware fact that just after having the experience of the class conflict a new political ideology was emerged which asked for the establishment of classless society and ultimately a political platform was made with a new political philosophy. Now we have seen two lines of political ideology i.e. left wing party and right wing party. This differentiation is based on their ideological principles. So, political party is established in order to manifest certain ideological principle for the welfare of the people as a whole.

It has already been mentioned above about the basic objective of a political party. It is a fact that the success of democratic principles is fully determined by the integrity and performance of the political party. Therefore political party has a big role in a society where the democratic principle and system is fully in operation. It is a known fact that every political party is established on the basic foundation of certain ideology. So one of the basic functions of a political party is to formulate a policy for the public. In the democracy the governance of the state is made through the public mandate. So, there is a stiff ideological and policy competition among the political parties. In order to make awareness among the people the party has set a policy and programme and it is reflected in their election manifesto. If the policies and programmes were welcomed by the people the party would be able to command the majority to the legislature and formed the government. Automatically the agendas placed for the approval of the common people would be implemented as a policy of the government. So to formulate of public policy is an important function of political parties.

To impart political education to the common people is also another function of the political party. The various key issues affecting the social, economic and political life of the common people is able to come to their knowledge only after having a platform for a free discussion. In a democratic society this platform is provided by the political party. Lack of knowledge or deliberate ignorance to the importance of the political party among the common people has created a serious factor for vitiates the political atmosphere in a country. Lack of interest of the people towards the political parties makes a very good room for self-seekers and manipulators to occupy the seat of authority. And it led to disaster of society. Therefore political party has a big role in the promotion of the society. In a democratic country the people are able to aware their interest and role mainly the active political campaign and propaganda during the time of election. On the other hand active participation of common people in the election also greatly helped the political parties in exercising their function very successfully.

In addition to this, another important function and duty of the political party is to see whether they are able to fulfill wishes and aspiration of the people which were promised to them at the time of election campaign. The beauty of democracy is that if the party who received the mandate of the people for the governance of the state fails to implement or fulfill the wishes of the people, they are thrown out at the time of next election. And the party is replaced by another to check the independent working their opponents.

To make an attempt to govern the state is the main objective of every political party, but they also have the role of an effective opposition political party if they are not able to get the mandate of the people. In democracy the role of the opposition political party is very important. A healthy democratic system could be possible only when opposition political parties discharge their constructive duties very effectively. To act the role as the watchdog of the government is also another duty of political party. As an opposition party they have to point out the undemocratic nature of the ruling party and to prevent from becoming despotic. So if the political parties discharge the function of an opposition, the healthy atmosphere in democratic principle will continue in a positive direction and people also will enjoy the fruit of it.

As a whole the main function of a political party is to make a channel of communication between the people and government. Through their platform the party always informed the government the wishes and desire of the people and their reader to the nature of the governance of the ruling party. At the same time they also keep the people inform about the various programme and healthy atmosphere in the democratic system by removing all the suspicious and distrust of the legitimacy of the democratic government.

Then in order to make it an effective political organisation the party has to fulfills certain criteria. These criteria are to be reflected in the constitution of the party. The ideology and agendas are the basic criteria of a political party. As has already been mentioned above about the background of the establishment of a political party. So, in order to find the people together the fundamental principles should be reflected in the constitution. Since political party may not be a loosely knit organisation of some people the views of all the members should be incorporates in the provision of the constitution. Over and above the party also should have a distinctive provision for the promotion of national interest from any type of communal line and its interest.

Political party is a leader producing organisation. In the democracy the leader or leaders of the political party would be the important elements to the governances of the country. It is mentioned that the leadership of a political party can be broadly categorizes into two i.e. public leaders and associational leader. Men who represent party as candidate for public office is regarded as public leader and men who confined in the organisatiional matter of the party is called associational leader. But there is no sharp differences between this two as men always moved him one to other and sometimes in party leaders also hold two positions.

These are the some basic characters which are to be possessed by every political party. From these above observations it can be suggested that the establishment of a political party is always associated with the history of the political environment of the state and its social and economic life. At the same time the proposed political party have to give a new ideas and agendas which are considered but for the welfare of the people.

In relation to this framework we can examine the nature and character of the Federal Party of Manipur in its process for the emergence as a political party.

It has already been mentioned above about the historical basis for the establishment of Federal Party of Manipur as a state level political organization. From this fact it is quite clear that this party was established with an objective to make an attempt to be one of the best alternative political platforms which could represent the basic feeling of the common people. After having a long experience of the nature of political attitude and working of the different political parties in the state a general impression was developed among the people that the existing political parties would not be able to protect the democratic value of the people. Their indulgence in so many activities like corruption, malpractices in the administration, failure in the safeguarding of the national interest, had created an impression among the people that the only interest of party worker or leader of any political organization was nothing but to work for their personal comfort in the name of democracy. In fact, the helpless persons were disgusted to see the party men. At same time the people also was not able to see the best alternative political system. They were not in favour of the feudal or any type of system that can check the basic right of the human being in a civilized society. This confusing situation was reached its zenith in the middle of nineteenth eighties. And the people of Manipur began to witness a serious type of political instability in the functioning of the governance of the state and ultimately the degree of mistrust between common people and persons in the political organization also reached to an explosive situation. When this was the situation, the idea for the establishment of a new political organizations, was emerged among the political and social thinkers. These are the historical backgrounds for the establishment of Federal Party of Manipur as a political party in the state.

While the idea for the establishment of a new political organization was emerged the total picture of the social and economic situations of the state was always kept in the minds of the members. Lack of opportunity for self generating economic condition was the main issue faced by the people and it also affects the whole the economic life of the state. The detail conditions have already been discussed in the previous chapters. The economic is the modern politics. Without economics concept and agendas no political party would be able to stand for a considerable period of time. In the case of the establishment of Federal Party of Manipur as a political organization the founder members always kept in their mind about the economic situation in Manipur which was developed just after the integration into India and this issue was always treated kept as a priority in their discussion. Ultimately they came to a conclusion that the parasitic culture in the field of economic life of the people of Manipur should be removed. This could be done only when there is a possibility of self- generating economic condition in Manipur. This idea was also categorically explained to the Government of India when the team of Finance Commission of India had visited Manipur. The possibilities to provide a big financial assistance as a means for the self-generating economic conditions of Manipur were also explored by the party. So the principle of sustainable economic development was also the basic policy of the party. In addition to this the social issue which is now prevailing in Manipur was also discussed during the course of the establishment of this party. It was a unanimous view of all the founder members of the organisation that since Manipur society is based on plural based society the interest of all the ethnic groups of people should be respected and well protected. At the same time they have also acknowledged the attempts of every ethnic group for the promotion of their cultural identity. On the basis of this political and social outlook they have also placed their view very categorically that every ethnic people should have the opportunity to foster and promote their cultural life. Keeping this view into consideration they invented the idea of 'Social Federalism' so that every group of people either big or small shall have the privilege to enjoy the equal opportunity to promote their cultural identity. This is the basic social policy and principle of the Federal Party of Manipur. From this fact it can be concluded that the establishment of this party was also based on the socio-economic condition of the state of Manipur.

Every political organization should have its own principles and ideology. The basic ideology of the new party should be different from the existing political parties. This was also exactly happened in the case of Federal Party of Manipur. The strength of this party was in her ideology. The party proposed the idea of 'Federalism' as a new political principle within the conceptual framework of democracy. It has already been mentioned in the previous chapter about the theoretical principle of federalism. The only objective of the party was that since Indian states and society is constituted on the basic foundation of the system of plural society the harmonious relationship could be possible only when the principle of the federalism is introduced. Actually the outlook of the party was based on national perspective. The practice of the centre and State relationship was the main framework for the emergence of the idea of federalism. The main ideology of the party was to introduce federalism and autonomy in the centre state relationship. Though it is very much in the constitution but still no party was able to point out this fact. This is the major contribution of Federal Party of Manipur in the political arena of Republic of India.

We have seen that the Federal Party of Manipur was established with a basic historical foundation. This party was established to promote and foster the national identity of the people of Manipur with a clear economic, social and cultural policy. Therefore that Federal Party of Manipur possessed all the requisite qualifications of being a progressive political organization. In short it Federal Party of Manipur was a regional party having a national outlook.

APPENDIX-I
Notice for Public Meeting
(4th October 1993)

It is hereby given for the general information that a PUBLIC MEETING will be held on Thursday, the 21st October 1993 at 10 a.m. at Majorkhul Community Hall. Imphal. All concerned are invited to attend the same.

AGENDA:

1. Establishment of a new regional political party in Manipur.
2. Election of ad hoc office bearers and Executive Members.
3. Formation of a Constitution Drafting Committee.
4. Misc.

Conveners

Sd/-
1. Dr. Jitendra Singh

Sd/-
2. Dr. N. Joykumar Singh

Sd/-
3. Dr. Vanlalnghak

Sd/-
4. Mr. Seipu Sitlhou

Sd/-
5. Mr Ashinpu Gangmei

Copy to:

All concerned

(For contact please-ring up
Telephone No. 223363)

Sd/-

(Dr. M. Jitendra Singh)

APPENDIX-II

Letter from Election Commission for the Registration of Party

ELECTION COMMISSION OF INDIA
Nirvachan Sadan,
Ashoka Road,
New Delhi-110001.

No.56/164/93/J.S.II Dated the 23rd December 1993.

To

Professor Gangmumei Kamei,
President,
Federal Party of Manipur,
Head Office: -GILEAD DEULAHLAND,
Imphal-795001 (Manipur).

Sub:- Federal Party of Manipur – Registration under section 29A of the Representation of the People Act, 1951, as a political party.

Sir,

I am directed to state that the Election Commission of India, after having considered your application, dated 10-11-93 for registration of Federal Party of Manipur as a political party and the documents produced in support of the statements/averments made/contained in the said application and the submissions made by Prof. Gangmumei

Kamei, President, Shri S. H. Seipu, General Secretary, M. Maringa, Vice President & Shri Alex, Executive Member of the party before the Commission on 22-12-1993 in respect of the said application, has registered the said party as a political party under section 29A of the Representation of the People Act, 1951 on and with effect from 22-12-1993.

2. As provided in sub-section (9) of 29A of the Representation of the People Act, 1951, the party shall communicate to the Commission without delay any change in its name, head office, office bearers, address or in any other material matters.

3. It may be noted that the registration will not entitle the party to the reservation of any exclusive symbol for it. However the candidates duly set up by the party at an election will be entitled to benefits of preference over independent candidates under paragraph 12 of the Election Symbols(Reservation and Allotment) Order, 1968.

Yours faithfully,

SOHAN LAL
Under Secy. (Legal)

No. 56/164/93/J.S. II Dated:- 23-12-1993.

Copy to the Chief Electoral Officers of all states and Union Territories (except Chief Electoral Officers of Jammu and Kashmir and West Bengal).

Sd/-
UNDERSECRETARY
(LEGAL)

APPENDIX-III

ELECTION COMMISSION OF INDIA

Nirvachan Sadan,
Ashoka Road
New Delhi-110 001

30th October 1995

NOTIFICATION

No. 56/95(10)—WHERAS the Election Commission of India has reviewed the poll performance of all political parties at the General Election to the Legilative Assembly of Manipur held in February-March, 1995, in term of paras 6 and 7 of the Election Symbols (Reservation and Allotment) Order, 1968; and

Whereas on such review the election Commission is satisfied that the Federal Party of Manipur a registered and unrecognized party, has become eligible for recognition as a state party in Manipur, in terms of para 6(2) of the election symbols (Reservation and Allotment) order 1968 and

Whereas , the election commission has decided to recognize the said Federal Party of Manipur as a State Parties Manipur and reserve the symbol "Rising Sun" for the said party in the said state.

Now Therefore, in pursuance of clause (b) (c) and (d) of sub-para (I) and sub-para (2) of paragragph 17 of the Election Symbols (Reservation and Allotment) Order, 1968, the Election Commission hereby makes the following further amendments to its Notification No.56/92 dated 07.01.1993 published as O.N. 2(E) in the Gazette of India, Extraordinary, part II, Section 3(iii) on 08.01.1993 and as amended from time to time, namely:-

(i) In TABLE-II of the said Notification:- Against the entry "Manipur" in column 1 the following entries shall be inserted in column 2,3 and 4- respectively:-

Table I

Sl. No.	**Name**	**Add.**	**Symbol allotted**
4.	Federal Party of Manipur	Majorkhul, Imphal, Pin-795001.	Rising Sun

(II) In Table-III of the said Notification, the entries under column 1 and 2 relating to " Federal Party of Manipur" ' mentioned at serial No. 332 shall be deleted:

(III) In Table IV of the said notification-

(i) against "14-Manipur" in column, the entry "19-Rising Sun" specified in column 2 shall be deleted;

By order

Ghanshyam Khohar, Secy.

APPENDIX IV

LIST OF OFFICIAL CANDIDATES OF FEDERAL PARTY OF MANIPUR FOR GENERAL ELECTION TO THE 6TH MANIPUR LEGISLATIVE ASSEMBLY 1995 AD .

Sl. No	**Name**	**Constituency**	**No. of A/C**	**District**
1.	Lairellakpam Lala Singh	Khundrakapam	1	Imphal East
2.	Wakambam Thoiba Singh	Heingang	2	-do-
3.	Hijam Heramot Singh	Thongju	5	-do-
4.	Kamei Shanahal	Lamlai	8	-do-
5.	Laikhuram Jayenta Kumar Singh	Thangmeiband	9	Imphal west
6.	Laishram Nanda Kumar Singh	Uripok	10	-do-
7.	Salam Damudor Singh	Sagolband	11	-do-
8.	Sougaijam Somorjit Singh	Yaiskul	14	-do-
9.	Oinam Shamu Singh	Wangkhei	15	Imphal East
10.	Ngaseppam Nimai Singh	Patsoi	19	Imphal West
11.	KhumbongMayum Dhruba Singh	Langthabal	20	-do-

(Condt.)

Sl. No	N… District	Constituency	No. of A/C	
12.	Yumanm Mani Singh	Wangoi	22	-do-
13.	Oinam Tombi Singh	Oinam	25	Bishnupur
14.	A.Brajamohon	Bishnupur	26	-do-
15.	K.Ningtampao	Jiribam	40	Imphal east
16.	L. Benjamin	Chanddel	41(ST)	Chandel
17.	K.Raina	Tadubi	49(ST)	Sanapati
18.	John	Saitu	51(ST)	Sadar hills
19.	Gangmumei Kamei	Nungba	54(ST)	Tamenglong
20.	Ms B.K Rose	Thanlon	56(ST)	Churachanpur
21.	Thangkhenkhup	Saikot	59(ST)	-do-
22.	Vungkholian	Shinghat	60(ST)	-do-

APPENDIX-V

List of official candidates of Federal Party of Manipur for General Election to the 7th Manipur Legislative Assembly 2000 A.D.

Sl. No.	Name	Constituency	No of A/C	District
1.	L. Sharatchandra Singh	Khundrakpam	1	Imphal east
2.	Dr. W. Thoiba	Heingang	2	-do-
3.	Th. Brajamani Singh	Kshetrigao	4	-do-
4.	S. Brajagopal Sharma	Thongju	5	-do-
5.	H. Nabachandra	Keirao	6	-do-
6.	MD Aziruddin	Andro	7	-do-
7.	Dr N. Sharatkumar Singh	Thangmeiband	9	Imphal west
8.	L. Nandakumar	Uripok	10	-do-
9.	S. Natum Singh	Sagolband	11	-do-
10.	L.Bheigachandra Singh	Keisamthong	12	-do-
11.	H. Rajen Sharma	Wangkhei	15	Imphal east
12.	W. Priyokumar Singh	Lamshang	17	-do-
13.	Nn. Nodia	Naoriya Pakhanglakpa	21	Imphal west

(Condt.)

Sl. No.	Name District	Constituency	No of A/C	
14.	MD Abdul karim	Mayang Imphal	23	-do-
15.	Salam Gopal	Moirang	27	Bishnupur district
16.	N. Ibobi Singh	Kumbi	29	-do-
17.	l. Kadamjit Singh	Wangkhei	32	Imphal east
18.	M. Jugeshwor Singh	Heirok	33	Thoubal district
19.	Kh. Maniton Singh	Wangjing Tentha	34	-do-
20.	M. Borajao	Khangabok	35	-do-
21.	MD. Basiruddin	Wabgai	36	-do-
22.	A. Sattar Yumkhaibam	Kakching	37	-do-
23.	N. Rajendro	Hiyanglam	38	-do-
24.	T. Leo kamchingthang	Chandel(ST)	41	Chandel district
25.	L.N. Mate	Tengnoupal(ST)	42	-do-
26.	S. Shimrei	Ukhrul(ST)	44	Ukhrul district
27.	Dr. Khasim Ruiva	Chingai(ST)	45	-do-
28.	Johanson keising	Saikul(ST)	46	Senapati
29.	P.S. Henri Paotei	Karong(ST)	47	-do-
30.	K. Rasina	Tadubi(ST)	49	-do-
31.	V Chonghoi	Kangpokpi(ST)	50	-do-
32.	Haokholet kipgen	Saiton(ST)	51	-do-
33.	Th. Athuan Abonmei	Tamei(ST)	52	Tamenglong
34.	Prof Gangmumei kamei	Nungba (ST)	54	-do-
35.	Dr. Vanlalnghak	Tipaimukh(ST)	55	Churachand-pur

(Condt.)

Sl. No.	Name District	Constituency	No of A/C	
36.	S. l. Soneimang Vaiphei	Henglep (ST)	57	-do-
37.	Mrs. Hathoi Buansing	Saikot (ST)	59	-do-
38.	Thangkhe khup	Singhat (ST)	60	-do-

APPENDIX-VI

List of the Candidates of Federal Party of Manipur for the 8th Assembly Election, 2002

Sl. No.	No. & Assembly Constituency	Name of the Candidates
1.	1 - Khundrakpam	K. Tomba Singh
2.	2 - Heingang	Dr. W. Thoiba Singh
3.	3 - Khurai	N. Bihari Singh
4.	4 - Kshetrigao	Ay. Deben Singh
5.	5 - Thongju	S. Brajagopal Sharma
6.	6 - Keirao	H. Bidur Singh
7.	7 - Andro	S. Chandra
8.	8 - Lamlai	Ksh. Biren Singh
9.	9 - Thangmeiband	Binoy Ningthoujam
10.	10 - Uripok	P. Achou Singh
11.	11 - Sagolband	M. Kumar Singh
12.	12 - Keishamthong	L. Ibomcha Singh
13.	13 - Singjamei	I. Hemochandra Singh
14.	15 - Wangkhei	A. Rajen Sharma

(Condt.)

Sl. No.	No. & Assembly Constituency	Name of the Candidates
15.	16 – Sekmai (SC)	N. Biren Singh
16.	17 - Lamshang	S. Rajen Singh
17.	18 - Konthoujam	Mahendra N.
18.	19 - Patsoi	L. Chandramani Singh
19.	20 - Langthabal	L. Memo Singh
20.	21 - Naoriya Pakhanglakpa	Ch Priyokumar Singh
21.	23 - Mayang Imphal	M. Nilachandra Singh
22.	27 - Moirang	S. Gopal
23.	28 - Thanga	S. Ibohal
24.	29 - Kumbi	Kh. Nabakumar
25.	30 - Lilong	Burhanuddin
26.	31 - Thou bal	L. Tomba Singh
27.	32 - Wangkhem	L. Kadamjit
28.	33 - Heirok	N. Sovakiran
29.	35 - Khangabok	L. Jatra Singh
30.	36 - Wabgai	Md. Basiruddin
31.	38 - Hiyanglam	M. Kunjosingh
32.	39 - Sugnu	M. Babu Singh
33.	40 - Jiribam	K. Sharat Singh
34.	43 - Phungyar (ST)	K. Somi
35.	44 - Ukhrul (ST)	As. Shimreiyo
36.	45 - Chingai (ST)	Dr. Khashim Ruivah
37.	46 - Saikul (ST)	Soineimang

(Condt.)

Sl. No.	No. & Assembly Constituency	Name of the Candidates
38.	47 - Karong (ST)	Ps. Henri Paotei
39.	48 - Mao (ST)	Soso Lorho
40.	49 - Tadubi (ST)	N Kayaisii
41.	50 - Kangpokpi (ST)	Thangminlien
42.	51 - Kaitu (ST)	Paseh
43.	53 - Tamenglong (ST)	Samuel Jendai
44.	54 - Nungba (ST)	Prof. Gangmumei Kamei
45.	55 - Tipaimukh (ST)	D.r Vanlalnghak
46.	57 - Henglep (ST)	Jainson Haokip
47.	59 - Saikot (ST)	D. Jangkhongam
48.	60 - Sing hat (ST)	N. Zatawn

BIBLIOGRAHY

'Application for registration as a Political Party' addressed to the Secretary, Election Commission of India, 10th November 1993.

'A BLUE PRINT FOR ECONOMIC REGENERATION OF MANIPUR' (Memorandum submitted to the 10th Finance Commission by Federal Party of Manipur, 8th April 1994.

'A PROPOSAL FOR FEDERALISM AND AUTONOMY IN INDIAN POLITY' (A memorandum submitted to Shri H. D. Deve Gowda, the Prime Minister of India. Imphal, 24th October 1996.

'A Review Of Urbanization Policy' (an occasional paper of Federal Economic Unit No. I) prepared by Jagat Thoudam, Convenor, Federal Economic Unit. November 1995.

Agenda of United Front Manipur 2000.

Constitution of Federal Party of Manipur. Published by FPM.

'Federal Party and the emergence of the United Front Ministry', press release of FPM, 24TH December 1997.

'FEDERAL PARTY OF MANIPUR': The Basic Issues. 'Federalism is the need of the hour'. Published by FPM.

Federal Agenda 1999: the manifesto of Federal Party of Manipur.

Federation and Autonomy for Manipur. Published by FPM.

Federalism in India by Prof. Gangmumei Kamei.

Financial Situation of Manipur: An analysis. Federal Party of Manipur, June 2000.

Letter from Shri Sohan Lal, Under Secretary (Legal), Election Commission of India to Prof. Gangmumei Kamei, President of FPM. No. 56/164/93/J.S. II/3019 of 23rd November 1993.

Letter from Prof. Gangmumei Kamei, President of FPM to Shri Sohan Lal, Under Secretary (Legal), Election Commission of India, dated 10th December 1993.

Letter from S.H Sheipu, General Secretary of FPM to the Secretary, Election Commission of India. No. FPM/RE/I/93-94 of 21ST December 1993.

Letter from Shri Sohan Lal, Under Secretary (Legal), Election Commission of India, to Prof. Gangmumei Kamei, President of FPM dated 23rd December 1993.

Letter from Topas Kumar, Under Secretary, Election Commission of India, to General Secretary of FPM No. 56/FPM/Review/95/J.S.II/497 of 31st July 1995.

Letter from Prof. Gangmumei Kamei, President of FPM to Shri H.D. Deve Gowda, the Prime Minister of India, 30th June 1996.

Letter from Prof. Gangmumei Kamei to the Chief Electoral Officer. No.FPM/Symbol/95 of 17th January 1995.

Memorandum submitted to Eleventh Finance Commission by the Federal Party of Manipur. Imphal, 18th May 1999.

Memorandum submitted to Shri H. D. Deve Gowda, the Prime Minister of India, 24th October 1996.

Memorandum submitted to Shri I.K. Gujaral, the Prime Minister of India by Federal Party of Manipur. Imphal, 22nd May 1997.

Memorandum submitted to Shri I.K. Gujaral the Prime Minister of India by all political parties of Manipur, 22nd May 1997.

Memorandum submitted to Shri Atal Bihari Vajpayee, the Prime Minister of India by Federal Party of Manipur, 21st May 1997.

Memorandum submitted to Shri Nitish Kumar, Union Agriculture Minister, by Peasant Front of Federal Party of Manipur on 13th September 2002.

Memorandum submitted to Shri Shiva Charan Das, Chairman, Parliamentary Standing Committee on Agriculture by Federal Party of Manipu,. 9th June 1997.

Notice for a PUBLIC MEETING. The 4th October 1993.

Notice of the General Assembly of Federal Party of Manipur dated 31st October 1993.

Proceeding of the Public Meeting held on 21st October 1993.

Presidential Address on Special Session of the General Assembly of Federal Party of Manipur, 9th November 1993.

Proceedings of the Special Session of the General Assembly of Federal Party of Manipur, 9th November 1993.

Proceedings of the resolutions of the 4th General Assembly of Federal Party of Manipur held on 1st May 2000.

'Presidential Address' at the 4th General Assembly of Federal Party of Manipur held on 1st May 2000.

'Press Statement' of United Democratic Front, 3rd July 1995.

'President's Speech to Federal Working Committee'. FPM Action Plan for General Election to Manipur Legislative Assembly, 1999. 10th April 1999.

'Presidential Address' on the 2nd Convention of Federal Party of Manipur 20-21 October 1995.

Proceedings of the Resolution of the 2nd Convention held on 20-21 October 1995.

Proceedings of the meeting of the FPM legislative party held on 14th February, 2001 with Prof. Gangmumei Kamei, President and leader of Legislative Party in the chair.

Statement on Governor's Address (Read out in the Assembly on 15th September 1995).

'Statement of FPM in its support to the Congress led Ministry' issued by the FPM.

'The memorandum submitted to the Governor of Manipur in connection with the withdrawal of support from the Congress led Ministry signed by nine MLAs, July 1995.

'TASK BEFORE US' an issue paper circulated by the party to the party workers for general discussion.14TH March 2001.

The Federal Agenda 2002 (Manifesto of FPM for 2002 election).

The Federal Agenda 1996: the manifesto of Federal Party of Manipur.

The Federal Manifesto 1995 (Federation is the need of the hour: Autonomy for our identity).

The Federal Approach and Autonomy for Manipur. Published by FPM, 1999.

INDEX

A

Additional Resource Mobilization (ARM), 93
Ambedkar, Dr. B.R., 14
Armed Forces Special Power Act 1958, 85, 88
Assembly demand co-ordination committee, 6
Autonomy for identity, 52
Autonomy for Manipur, 20, 24-26

B

Ball, Alan K., 116
Basic issues, 20, 26
Basic Minimum Service (BMS), 98
Black Draconian Laws, 85
Burk, Edmunf, 115

C

Capitalism, 23
Capitalistic, 17
Central government, 22
Chandramani, L., 110
Chauvinistic, 17
Common minimum programme, 73
Communist Party, 12
Conceptual principle the party, 59
Concurrent list, 84
Congress (I) in Manipur, 32
Congress Legislature Party, 60
Congress Party, 11, 12, 43, 59, 105, 117
Constitution, 37
Constitutional Drafting Committee, 34
Corruption, 121
Cultural Integration Conference, 31

D

Democratic people alliance, 108
Democratic revolutionary movement, 40
Dena, Lal, 32
Development works, 74
Devi, L. Sorojini, 70
District Committee, 38
Draft Constitution, 38
Dream of the self-sufficiency, 22

E

Economic policy, 7
Economic position of Manipur, 6, 22
Economic stagnancy, 15, 20, 22-24

Educated unemployment people, 8
Election campaign, 78
Election Commission, 40, 41, 55, 69
Election symbol for party, 40
Election symbol (Reservation and Allotment) Order 1968, 56
Element of population, 95
Eminent citizens, 88
England, 117
Establishment of responsible government, 2
Ethnic line in the hill area, 12
Ethnic pluralism, 20, 21-22

F

Federal Party of Manipur (FPM), 2-3, 29, 35, 46, 49, 61, 73, 88-90, 99, 105, 110, 121, 122, 123
Federating states, 20
Finance and currency central legislative affairs, 45
Finance Commission, 46, 98
Financial assistance, 97
Financial bankruptcy, 7
First convention of 1994, 52
Flag of the party, 40
Frontal organizations and cells of the party, 38
Frontrunner, 105-114
Fundamental right, 14

G

General body, 38
General election, 112
  of 1995, 63
Gilchrist, 115
Gowda, H.D. Deva, 83, 84, 98
Grievances and problems, 38
Growth of political consciousness, 1
Gujral, Indrakumar, 86

H

Haokholet Kipgen of Saitu (ST) Assembly Constituency, 106
Human rights, 10
Human Rights Commission, 48

I

Ideological principles, 10
Independent MLA, 61
Indian Constitution, 13, 14, 45, 47, 51, 53, 82
Indian federation, 13
Indian suzerainty, 4
Instrument of Accession Act, 4, 25
Insurgencies and revolution, 20, 24
Integration of Manipur into India, 24
Integration of Manipur, 5
Intellectuals, 16
Inter-Ethnic Council in Manipur, 48, 54, 65
Internal colonialism, 8
Inter-party bureaucracy, 112
Involvement in public issues, 81-103
  autonomy for the state of Manipur, 83-89
  developmental issues, 98-103
  economic, 89-90
  Finance Commission, 90-98

general arguments and observations, 96
observations, 96
political, 81-83

J

Jammu and Kashmir, 47
Janata Dal, 61
Job facilities, 6

K

Kamei, Gaidon, 70
Kamei, Gangmumei, 31, 58, 75, 82, 89, 107
Kanglei League, Manipur Hill Union (MHU), 2
Kapur, A.C., 14
Kashmir, 84
Keishing, Rishang, 61, 72
Kendra Committee, 38
Kipgen, Haokholet, 76
Krishak Sabha, 12
Kukis, 21
Kuki-Naga conflict, 61
Kuki National Assembly (KNA), 2, 12
Kuki-Zomi clash, 73
Kumar, Nitish, 101

L

Law enforcing machineries, 16
Legislature, 2
Legitimization of the organisation, 34-56
convention of the party 1994, 42-51
autonomy of the state of Manipur, 46
body of the resolution, 42
economic resolutions, 48
equal representation of the states in the parliament, 44
more power for the state, 45-46
resolution on social federalism, 49
formal recognition and allotment of symbol, 55-56
general election of 1995, 51-55
nature of proposed draft constitution, 36-41
objectives, 36
presentation of draft constitution, 34
provisional registration, 41-42
reservation of symbol, 42
Leviathan, 43
Lohri, O., 68
Loktak down stream, 74
Loktak Hydro Electric Project, 102
Loktak project, 64

M

Maharaja of Manipur, 4
Maharaja, 2
Majorkhul Community Hall, 19
Mandate of the people, 75
Manifesto the united front, 73
Manipur autonomy, 25
Manipur Hill People Regulation, 1947, 47
Manipur in Indian Federation, 20-21

Manipur National Union, 12
Manipur People Party (MPP), 2, 12
Manipur State Congress Party (MSCP), 11, 67, 73, 75
Manipur State Constitution Act 1947, 5, 44, 47, 64, 83
Maringa, M., 32, 41
Meitei, 21
Meitei Mayek, 71
Meitei Pangal, 21
Members of the office, 30
Merger agreement, 4
Merger of Mahipur into India, 2, 3, 10
MW heavy fuel based power project, 74

N

Naga, 21
Nagaland, 84
National games in Manipur, 74
National Super Highway Project, 100
National Union, 12
Nationalist Socialist Democratic Party (NSDP), 2, 12
NDA government, 108
Neo-colonialism, 15
New Economic Policy (NEP), 91, 93
New economic policy, 7
Nikhil Hindu Manipuri Mahasabha, 1, 2
Nikhil Manipuri Mahasabha, 12
NNP, 61
Non-Manipuri people, 6, 11, 21
Non-violent type of political movement, 16
North Eastern Region (NER), 98
NSCN (IM), 109

O

Objectives of political parties, 26-27
Outbreak of serious violation, 10

P

Pan-Manipuri identity, 1
Pant, K.C., 94
Paojel, 19
Parliamentary democracy, 15
Participation in the governance, 58-71
  formation of united front ministry 1997, 67
  parliamentary election of 1999, 70
    1996, 62
  participation in ministry formation, 58
  state assembly election 2000, 72
Parturition, 19-33
  background of leaders, 30
Party worker, 121
Paswan, Ram Villas, 87
People front, 106
Planning commission, 64
Political activities, 16
Political and economic conditions, 9
Political education, 118
Political party, 115
Political status of a Part C, 5

Post-election scenario, 58
Power and function of the office functionary, 39
Praja Mandol, 12
Praja Sangha, 12
Praja Sanmeloni, 12
Praja Shanti, 12
Praja Socialist Party (PSP), 2, 11
Preamble of the Constitution, 36
Prelude, 1-17
Pre-Merger State Constitution Act 1947, 83
Primary unit, 38
Principle of transparency, 4
Private enterprises, 6
Progressive Janata, 61
Pro-merger group, 4
Public leader, 120
Public policy, 118
Punjab Security Act, 54

R

Raina, K., 107, 108
Raina, K., 77
Regional issues, 17
Relation between federal government and Manipur state, 26
Relationship between Indian and Myanmar, 49
Representation of the People Act 1951, 41
Resolution of the public meeting, 28
Resolution on the formation of Federal Party of Manipur, 28
Restructure on Indian polity, 85
Revolution, 20
Revolutionary movements, 9, 15
Ruivah, Khasim, 76
Ruling party, 120

S

Samata Party, 61
Sarkaria Commission, 25, 84
Seipu, S.H., 32, 41
Self-generating employment, 8
Shaiza, Shimrio, 66
Sharma, Brajagopal, 107
Singh, Charan, 102
Singh, Hijam Irabot, 12
Singh, Kumar, 32
Singh, L. Bhagyachandra, 76, 77, 78
Singh, L. Jayenta, 106
Singh, M. Jitendra, 33
Singh, N. Chittaranjan, 66, 68
Singh, N. Joykumar, 32, 36, 39, 76, 94, 95
Singh, N. Pahari, 62
Singh, N. Sarat, 110
Singh, Naorem Birendra-kumar, 19
Singh, Nimai, 32, 34
Singh, Ranbir, 61
Singh, W. Nipamacha, 67, 101
Singh, W. Thoiba, 58, 76, 107, 108
Sixth general election, 58
Social development, 7
Social federalism, 21-22, 50, 63, 98, 123

Social justice, 63
Socialist Party, 12
Solution of revolutionary movements, 53
Special general body, 34, 40
Stand still agreement, 25
Stand still agreement, 4
State Human Rights Commission, 61
State List, 84
State Public Sector Understanding (SPSU), 97
Symbol of Rising Sun to FPM, 56

T

TADA, 54
Tadubi assembly constituency, 68, 69
Tenth Finance Commission, 90
Tourism affairs, 50a
Tragedy, 24

U

Union of states irrespective of population, 82
Union public service, 45
United Front Ministry, 105
United Legislative Front (ULF), 61, 67
Unity and territorial integrity, 74

V

Vajpayee, Atal Behari, 100
Valalnghak, Van, 33
Vanlalnghak, 36
Violent type of political movement, 16

W

Women Commission, 72

X

Yumnam, Amar, 90

Z

Zilla Parishad, 47
Zomi, 73

□□□